Cambridge Elements ≡

Elements in Earth System Governance
edited by
Frank Biermann
Utrecht University
Aarti Gupta
Wageningen University
Michael Mason
London School of Economics and Political Science (LSE)

CHANGING OUR WAYS

Behaviour Change and the Climate Crisis

Peter Newell
University of Sussex

Freddie Daley
University of Sussex

Michelle Twena
University of Sussex

CAMBRIDGE
UNIVERSITY PRESS

CAMBRIDGE
UNIVERSITY PRESS

University Printing House, Cambridge CB2 8BS, United Kingdom

One Liberty Plaza, 20th Floor, New York, NY 10006, USA

477 Williamstown Road, Port Melbourne, VIC 3207, Australia

314–321, 3rd Floor, Plot 3, Splendor Forum, Jasola District Centre,
New Delhi – 110025, India

103 Penang Road, #05–06/07, Visioncrest Commercial, Singapore 238467

Cambridge University Press is part of the University of Cambridge.

It furthers the University's mission by disseminating knowledge in the pursuit of
education, learning, and research at the highest international levels of excellence.

www.cambridge.org
Information on this title: www.cambridge.org/9781009108492
DOI: 10.1017/9781009104401

First published 2022

A catalogue record for this publication is available from the British Library.

ISBN 978-1-009-10849-2 Paperback
ISSN 2631-7818 (online)
ISSN 2631-780X (print)

Changing Our Ways

Behaviour Change and the Climate Crisis

Elements in Earth System Governance

DOI: 10.1017/9781009104401
First published online: March 2022

Peter Newell
University of Sussex

Freddie Daley
University of Sussex

Michelle Twena
University of Sussex

Author for correspondence: Peter Newell, P.J.Newell@sussex.ac.uk

Abstract: In this Element, the authors develop an account of the role of behaviour change that is more political and social by bringing questions of power and social justice to the heart of their enquiry in order to appreciate how questions of responsibility and agency are unevenly distributed within and between societies. The result is a more holistic understanding of behaviour, as just one node within an ecosystem of transformation that bridges the individual and systemic. Their account is more attentive to questions of governance and the processes of collective steering necessary to facilitate large-scale change across a diversity of actors, sectors, and regions than the dominant emphasis on individuals and households. It is also more historical in its approach, looking critically at the relevance of historical parallels regarding large-scale behaviour change and what might be learned and applied to the contemporary context.

Keywords: behaviour change, climate change, politics, governance, social justice

ISBNs: 9781009108492 (PB), 9781009104401 (OC)
ISSNs: 2631-7818 (online), 2631-780X (print)

Contents

1 Introduction: Changing Our Ways   1

2 The Challenge of Scaling   17

3 Understanding Behaviour Change   29

4 Leverage and Tipping Points   43

5 Future Intervention Points   52

6 Conclusion   70

List of Abbreviations   73

References   74

1 Introduction: Changing Our Ways

What is the role of behaviour change in addressing the climate crisis? Sustainable behaviour change is rapidly rising up the climate policy agenda as many governments, cities, and corporations look to bolster the ambition and effectiveness of their climate policies.[1] After a long period where global climate policy predominantly focused on economic and technological initiatives, international bodies increasingly recognise the importance of behaviour change as part of broader efforts to achieve the Paris Agreement goal of restricting global warming to well below 2°C and aiming to halt temperatures at 1.5°C. The Intergovernmental Panel on Climate Change (IPCC), United Nations Environment Programme (UNEP) Emissions Gap report, and many models of how to achieve ambitious climate goals, now include the role of behaviour change.

Yet how to scale it in line with these targets remains a neglected topic. *Scaling* behaviour change requires a broader understanding of behaviours as collective, social, political, and cultural, and not just individual and economic: reducible to the sum of discrete consumption practices and 'choices' in the market. Understanding the everyday practices of governments, cities, corporations, and other social actors as forms of behaviour helps to reveal the interconnected nature of change where individual acts, however seemingly atomised, are never undertaken in isolation from the contexts in which they take place, impact upon, and which shape them. It takes us beyond the false binary of individual and system change. Moving from the individual and household 'outwards' as an additive approach to scaling will not achieve change at the speed and scale required if it neglects the drivers of consumption: the creation of demand, the embedding of cultural values and norms, and the relations of power that normalise and benefit from unsustainable consumption. Addressing these issues offers scope for more transformative change across society while addressing the inequities that leave the majority without access to basic goods and services and a minority over-consuming them.

Even when behaviour change is integrated into climate policy discourses, it is often treated in isolation from the underlying political and social forces driving fossil fuel consumption. We argue in this Element that production and consumption need to be better integrated in order to unlock the social transformation necessary to secure a low-carbon future. To do this, we suggest that scaling

---

[1] To be clear, 'sustainable behaviour change' refers to the need for behaviours to be more sustainable and in our case with particular reference to the need for radical decarbonisation. It should not be confused with sustaining current behaviours and hence frustrating attempts to change behaviours.

change needs to use all levers and tools within an ecosystem of transformation. Which tools and strategies are available to whom will depend on social and economic hierarchies and inequities, as well as the diverse contexts in which change is sought. We do not proffer one overarching theory of change here but rather draw on insights from a range of academic scholarship and the experience of practitioners to suggest useful intervention points for scaling change in line with the goals of the Paris Agreement. However, we are steadfast in our view that the privilege of choosing between systems change and individual change has long since passed. It is a false binary, and we now need both. Fostering a more holistic understanding of sustainable behaviour change that bridges both system and individual is foundational for scaling the transformative change we need to see.

Background

Behaviours change. That much we know. And if we were in any doubt about the speed with which they can change, the scale of their effects, the COVID-19 pandemic has served as a sharp reminder. But the COVID crisis has also revealed the deep inequalities that run through, within and between societies and the disproportionately adverse consequences faced by society's most vulnerable communities, highlighting how critical it is that transitions are grounded in social justice. Beyond such times of crisis, behaviours also change at key moments in our lives, when we have children, retire, or move home. They are shaped by a range of family, community, regional, and broader societal influences, as well as physical infrastructures. But there is little consensus about how best to deliberately shape and directly influence everyday behaviours around transport, food, and energy use in more sustainable directions and where *responsibility* and *agency* to affect that change lie.

Added to this, in the wake of the Paris Agreement and the IPCC's Special Report (2018) on the impacts of global warming, there is renewed attention to the question of the speed and scale of change, given that keeping within a 1.5°C rise will entail halving greenhouse gas (GHG) emissions by 2030. Published in autumn 2018, adopting language more associated with radicals and revolutionaries, the IPCC, often criticised for being cautious, called for 'transformative systemic change' to achieve the goals of the Paris Agreement (IPCC, 2018). It indicated the need for change across all sectors and regions of the world at unprecedented speed and called for behaviour change by all actors, alongside demand-side management, as crucial elements of this transformation. This message was underscored by the 2020 UN Emissions Gap report, which included a dedicated chapter on the role of equitable low-carbon lifestyles for the first time in the report's history (UNEP, 2020).

New ground has also been broken with the *1.5-Degree Lifestyles: Targets and Options for Reducing Lifestyle Carbon Footprints* report, which makes for sobering reading (Akenji et al., 2019). The study assessed GHG emissions-reduction potential by looking at lifestyle carbon footprints, defined as emissions both directly and indirectly induced from household consumption. It highlights the need for reductions of over 90 per cent in GHG emissions by 2050 from today's lifestyles. This implies per-person carbon footprint targets of 2.5 (tCO2e) in 2030, 1.4 by 2040, and 0.7 by 2050. To put these figures in context, allowing for differential impacts and uneven historical responsibility, this means footprints in developed countries will need to be reduced by between 80 and 93 per cent by 2050, assuming that actions for a 58–76 per cent reduction start immediately to achieve the 2030 target. Yet, even for developing countries, the report highlights the need to reduce footprints by 23–84 per cent, depending on the country and the scenario, by 2050. These required emission reductions obviously reflect very different starting points in terms of existing levels of consumption.

Despite its huge potential, sustainable behaviour change has not traditionally been given high priority in climate policy strategies and is often downplayed in debates about mitigation. In the international climate policy arena, it has often been neglected and overshadowed by a focus on technology and market mechanisms. This has side-lined a greater focus on changing consumption and demand-side options. We argue instead that we need both 'arms of the scissors' to achieve change at scale: limits on *supply* (of fossil fuels) and drastic reductions in *demand* (where behaviour change has an important role to play) (Green & Dennis, 2018). The idea that sustainable behaviour requires changes at both the individual and political levels and that these two areas are not only linked but also reinforce one another is slowly gaining traction (UNEP, 2020; Leventon et al., 2021). The 2019 *1.5-degree Lifestyles* report states: 'the sheer magnitude of change required for a shift towards 1.5-degree lifestyles can only be achieved through a combination of system-wide changes and a groundswell of actions from individuals and households' (Akenji et al., 2019).

Lifestyles can be targeted 'from above' through policies and attempts to shape infrastructures and choice architectures, as well as emerge organically 'from below' from autonomous actions on the part of civil society and households. This implies a combination of cultural change and shifting social norms, alongside interventions by institutions and through the market as part of what we call a broad 'ecosystem of transformation'. It suggests the need for understanding pathways to change, which combine top-down and bottom-up, state, market, and civil society-led transformations depending on the contexts in which they will be deployed (Scoones et al., 2015). The challenge of governing, steering, and coordinating behaviour change through these different pathways and via these different intervention points should not be underestimated and requires further attention from scholars of politics, international relations, and earth systems governance.

The recent turn towards behaviour change by international bodies is to be welcomed. In their 1.5°C report published in 2018, the IPCC noted with 'high confidence' that 'pathways that include low energy demand . . ., low material consumption, and low GHG-intensive food consumption have the most pronounced synergies and the lowest number of trade-offs with respect to sustainable development' (IPCC, 2018: 21). Likewise, in the latest World Energy Outlook, a scenario for primary energy demand imagines falls of 17 per cent between 2019 and 2030, even though the global economy is projected to be twice as large where 'electrification, efficiency gains and behaviour changes are central to achieving this' (IEA, 2020). The 2020 UN Emissions Gap report, meanwhile, calls for 'reforming consumption behaviour', noting that although

> two-thirds of global emissions are linked to private households, when using consumption-based accounting . . . The wealthy bear the greatest responsibility in this area. The combined emissions of the richest 1 per cent of the global population account for more than twice the combined emissions of the poorest 50 per cent. This elite will need to reduce their footprint by a factor of 30 to stay in line with the Paris Agreement targets. (UNEP, 2020: xxiv, xiii)

Given the scale and depth of required change in behaviours across society, but most especially among richer and more powerful social groups, it is unsurprising that politicians are not clamouring to reflect on, let alone act upon, the political, economic, social, and cultural implications of this. As President Bush Snr. famously stated at the Rio conference back in 1992, 'The American way of life is not up for negotiation'. Yet we present the case in this Element that it is a way of life increasingly emulated and pursued the world over that very much needs to be re-negotiated if further climate chaos is to be avoided.

Incremental transitions in the provision of services around energy, food, or transportation are no longer up to the scale of the challenge (Bataille et al., 2016; Zhang & Zhang, 2021). Deep decarbonisation across all sectors of the economy and wider social transformations are now required. With regard to behaviour change, this implies steering dramatic change across energy, food, and transport systems, where traditional governance systems often have limited direct reach and where powerful incumbent actors seek to preserve the status quo, as scholars of earth system governance increasingly recognise (Biermann, 2020).

Coordinating change within and across societies – and doing so in ways that account for significant inequalities – presents an unprecedented challenge for humanity. Perhaps most significantly, successfully addressing this challenge means countering the dominant organisation of the political economy in relation to income, work, and wealth generation and consumption. It touches, in other words, on the core of how capitalist economies are run.

For this reason, as we will explore in Section 3, existing scholarship is only partially helpful in understanding and engaging with these dynamics. Literature on behaviour change is often siloed into individual approaches to behaviour change (from economics and psychology) or more systemic approaches (from sociology and political economy): a divide we seek to bridge by exploring the interrelationship between individual and system change. Studies that model 1.5-degree compatible lifestyles (Akenji et al., 2021) are often technical in nature and have yet to explore the political and social challenges of enabling sustainable lifestyles. Despite a growing academic literature on behaviour change from economics (Thaler & Sunstein, 2009), sociology (Shove et al., 2012), psychology (Whitmarsh, 2009; Kasser, 2016), science and technology studies (Dubois et al., 2019), and politics (Princen et al., 2002; Dauvergne, 2008; Fuchs et al., 2016), there has been less attention to the question of scalability: key points of leverage and traction that bring about shifts of the scale and speed required to tackle the climate emergency.

How Important Is Behaviour Change?

Where behaviour change should sit within this broader landscape is subject to dispute, despite growing acceptance of its importance and potential impact in policy circles. Many recognise that it is an important dimension of responding effectively to the urgent threat of climate change, but views are often sharply divided on its significance relative to other drivers of emissions, such as energy infrastructures, for example, as well as on how to successfully initiate and sustain such shifts in behaviour across different contexts simultaneously. On the one hand, there are those who see it as a key site of change both in terms of direct and indirect effects on emissions from households' consumer choices, and more broadly in terms of the licence it gives governments and businesses to be more ambitious in their climate policies (Capstick et al., 2015; Dubois et al., 2019). On the other, there are real concerns about placing the burden for societal change on individual shoulders, where agency is often limited, and scapegoating can lead to backlash, disengagement, and denial, rather than positive engagement from citizens (Shove et al., 2012; Weintrobe, 2013). Indeed, individualising responsibility overlooks the huge inequalities in emissions between and within countries, where the lifestyles of the most affluent have a disproportionate impact, as we explore in Section 2.

There is also significant disagreement about how best to scale behaviour change. Government policy, economic incentives, and broader cultural change all have a role to play. But can they achieve the scale of change in the short term within which 'transformative action' needs to take place to meet the goals of the Paris Agreement? In climate and broader sustainability terms, some behaviours matter more than others. Carbon footprints are closely correlated with income levels, highlighting the need for targeted, differential, and contextualised strategies within and between societies and the adoption of strategies that simultaneously address wealth and inequality. Tools, strategies, levers, and entry points, to be effective, must recognise important cultural differences, uneven capacity to affect and enact change, and very different levels of responsibility. There are few one-size-fits-all solutions to delivering change at this scale across and between divided and unequal societies. Multipronged approaches are required across different sites and scales of governance. Robust evidence on the role of behavioural change in societal system transformations and empirical evidence of effective leverage points for societal change are needed to guide high-impact and scalable interventions from a range of actors for rapid changes towards sustainable human development. Yet clearly attributing agency and responsibility is a fraught and controversial exercise, and different parameters and benchmarks generate very different estimates about behaviours and the scope to change them.

Underlying the case for a bottom-up, behaviour change approach is the argument that a significant proportion, if not the majority, of emissions is ultimately derived from the consumption choices of individuals. For example, according to some estimates, households are responsible for 72 per cent of global GHG emissions as a result of their consumption behaviour (Hertwich & Peters, 2009). Ivanova et al. similarly show that around two-thirds of global GHG emissions are 'directly and indirectly' related to household consumption, where the global average is about 6 tCO2eq/cap (2020:1). An interdisciplinary study of 17 action types concluded that the implementation of the most successful behavioural programmes could reduce household carbon emissions in the USA by 20 per cent, an amount equal to the total annual emissions of France (Dietz et al., 2009). Measures such as avoiding eating meat or reducing air travel alone can bring about savings of as much as 15 billion tonnes (gigatons) by 2060 (Cafaro, 2011).

Focussing on low energy demand pathways, Grubler et al. explore an alternative mitigation scenario that includes lifestyle changes, accelerated adoption of renewable energy, agricultural intensification, and lab-grown meat (2018).

These reduce overall energy demand by 40 per cent from today's levels, which in turn reduces the burden on overall supply and makes it possible to reach the 1.5-degree target – as well as sustainable development goals (SDGs) – without the need to rely on negative emissions technologies (Grubler et al., 2018). Furthermore, van Vuuren et al. found that by combining lifestyle change, reduction of other greenhouse gases, and rapid electrification through renewable energy, it was possible to reduce, but not eliminate, the use of carbon dioxide removal (CDR) technologies (2018). From this perspective, individual behaviour undoubtedly drives both energy-intensive lifestyles and a large share of global carbon emissions and is also a potential source of large, low-cost emission reductions (Stern et al., 2016). This makes it a critical factor in achieving the 1.5°C goal under the Paris Agreement.

Others are more critical about such estimates because they include the entire lifecycle of the consumption of goods and services, from cradle to grave, and give consumers full responsibility for emissions, regardless of whether or not they are actually in a position to influence the supply chain and production process. The effect is to allocate a much higher share of environmental impacts to households than they will be able to actively influence. Yet, despite their limitations, these estimates do inform climate action plans. A report by Williamson et al. (2018), building on the earlier 'Drawdown' plan (2020), identifies and ranks 30 (of the original 80) 'Drawdown recommendations' that are dependent upon behaviour changes at the individual level. They categorise the recommendations into four domains: food, agriculture and land management, transportation, and energy and materials. The top recommendations include (1) reducing food waste, (2) plant-rich diets, (3) electric vehicles, and (4) rooftop solar. When taken together, it is estimated the thirty actions could mitigate 19.9 to 36.8 per cent of global emissions between 2020 and 2050 (Williamson et al., 2018). The *1.5-Degree Lifestyle* report also emphasises reducing meat and dairy consumption, switching to non-fossil-based energy, and reducing car use and air travel, and calculates that when combined, food, housing, and transportation comprise approximately 75 per cent of total carbon footprints (Akenji et al., 2019). While these studies point to the huge potential of behaviour change to achieve the aims of the Paris Agreement, the means of realising these potential contributions are less well understood.

A policy can affect such change through a range of tools that include regulation, the provision of infrastructure, market mechanisms and financial rewards (Hardman et al., 2017), and public-facing information campaigns targeted at a range of sectors. For example, this will include support to more plant-based diets, given that the report makes clear that livestock are responsible for more GHG emissions than all other food sources (up to 14.5 per cent of global GHG emissions). Globally, savings of carbon dioxide (CO_2) equivalent of between 29 and 70 per cent are possible by moving towards a more plant-based diet including measures aimed at reducing the demand for meat and other livestock products, bringing other co-benefits such as reducing consumption in line with human health guidelines (Willett et al., 2019). Likewise, efforts to reduce food waste need to be stepped up given the climate impacts of food production, of which a third currently gets wasted (FAO, 2011, 2019).

For industry, depending on the industrial sector, mitigation consistent with 1.5°C would mean a reduction of final energy demand by one-third, an increase of the rate of recycling of materials, and the development of a circular economy (IPCC, 2018: 335). There remains huge untapped potential to realise gains in energy efficiency and energy conservation. In the transport sector, for example, pricing and regulatory policies have successfully brought about change in places as diverse as Singapore, Stockholm, and London, where car ownership, car use, and GHG emissions have all been reduced (IPCC, 2018: 366). Notably, positive momentum can be brought about as co-benefits around health, air quality, and financial savings become apparent.

The debate about behaviour change often gets narrowed down to individual actions or what critics refer to as the individualisation of responsibility (Maniates, 2001). The parameters of what counts as a sustainable lifestyle are, therefore, contested. Getting a clear metric is a challenging task. At the level of principles and aims, Akenji and Chen (2016: 3) suggest, 'A "sustainable lifestyle" is a cluster of habits and patterns of behaviour embedded in a society and facilitated by institutions, norms and infrastructures that frame individual choice, in order to minimize the use of natural resources and generation of wastes, while supporting fairness and prosperity for all'. In Section 2, we discuss a range of approaches from 'One Planet Living' to sustainable consumption corridors, many inspired by the need to 'shrink and share': establishing upper limits on consumption and minimal thresholds to ensure the developmental needs of all are adequately met. This is not just about climate change, therefore, as efforts to radically decarbonise through behaviour change need to be cognisant of their impact on other environmental problems such as biodiversity loss, waste, and water pollution, where a narrow focus on decarbonisation may obscure unintended consequences if a more holistic approach is not taken. This might be the case, for example, with regard to the electrification of transport (without considering the intensification of mining for lithium and cobalt) and moves to plant-based diets (if pursued through monoculture industrial agriculture), for example, while noting that a failure to tackle climate change will render most SDGs impossible to achieve.

Although behaviour change is often assumed to be voluntary, we need to constantly recognise the changing circumstances that give rise to it where an appreciation of socially bounded agency and context is critical. The responsibility for societal transformations cannot be put on the sum of all individual shoulders. Such transformations can only be achieved when embedded in sustainable systems change, integrating shifts from individual values and community behaviour with societal changes in institutions and governance. It is choice architectures and systems of provision that are key. Indeed, the role of behavioural and value change provokes mixed reactions in environmental debates. Mary Heglar puts it bluntly,

> The belief that this enormous, existential problem could have been fixed if all of us had just tweaked our consumptive habits is not only preposterous; it's dangerous. It turns environmentalism into an individual choice defined as sin or virtue, convicting those who don't or can't uphold these ethics . . .. While we're busy testing each other's purity, we let the government and industries – the authors of said devastation – off the hook completely. This overemphasis on individual action shames people for their everyday activities, things they can barely avoid doing because of the fossil fuel-dependent system they were born into . . . Fight the oil and gas industry instead. (Heglar, 2019)

Even advocates of the significance of individual and household behaviour change recognise the limits of approaches that rely on that strategy alone. Dubois et al. suggest that 'short term voluntary efforts will not be sufficient by themselves to reach the drastic reductions needed to achieve the 1.5°C goal; instead, households need a regulatory framework supporting their behavioural changes. But there is also a mismatch between the roles and responsibilities conveyed by current climate policies and household perceptions of responsibility' (2019: 144). This reinforces our central argument about the importance of challenging these binaries and linking individual and system change as part of ecosystems of transformation.

Despite this, many policy approaches embody this disconnect and are built upon what Shove calls 'ABC' models of behaviour change (Cabinet Office, 2011), in which attitudes (A), drive behaviour (B), and hence choices (C) (Shove, 2010). Typically, 'individuals do not consciously decide to emit carbon. Rather, emissions are associated with the practices and routines of everyday life, from cooking to travelling' (Newell et al., 2015: 527). The routines of daily life are often embedded in the use of technologies, materials, and systems, which individuals have little power to alter, and that create a degree of lock-in (Unruh, 2000). This means going beyond 'expressions of individual preference and choice' to open up discussions about the very definition of 'taken for granted needs and the different means by which warmth and welfare, freedom and mobility, and economic and energy security might be achieved in different settings' (Newell et al., 2015: 527). The generation of demand and desire, everyday routines and practices, and the ways these are sedimented by regulations, social pressure, and built infrastructures all require greater attention.

Influencing Behaviour Change

Over the last three decades, there has been a plethora of initiatives targeted at individuals and households aimed at shifting behaviours to address the climate crisis and other sustainability challenges. Strategies by governments, corporations, and non-governmental organisations have included regulatory measures, market mechanisms, and interventions aimed at shifting behaviours and norms through education and public information campaigns, for example.

Yet gaps remain in our understanding of the complex ways in which individual behaviours are influenced and which interventions work best, which different disciplines have sought to fill using a broad range of methods and theories (which we explore in Section 3). As Vandenbergh and Sovacool (2016: 93) put it: 'A recent renewed focus on individual behaviour reflects the growing recognition that additional emission reductions from large, industrial sources would be expensive and inadequate to achieve many pollution standards and that individuals often contribute more emissions than the industrial sector, if viewed as a discrete source category'. It also flows from growing understanding of the influence of norms on environmental behaviours (Carlson, 2005; Doherty & Webler, 2016). This, more socially informed analysis, of everyday decision-making departs from and challenges conventional accounts of economic rationality (Vandenbergh & Sovacool, 2016). It strengthens an appreciation of social context by emphasising things like the size of the home and the demographics of who lives there (Tukker et al., 2010; Sovacool et al., 2018), the different key phases of life when particularly significant household decisions are made, such as when having children or retiring, and the role of regulation in supporting households in going beyond short-term voluntary actions (Dubois et al., 2019: 144; see also Girod et al., 2014).

Recognising the pace and scale of the sustainability transitions now required, this is a key moment to consolidate knowledge, evidence, and insights about the role of behavioural change in contributing to societal system transformations. It is also an opportune moment to contextualise and globalise the conversation about scaling behaviour change across cultures and regions and to look at the interface with different social cleavages and dynamics such as race, class, and gender. The focus to date has been on behaviour change in richer societies for obvious reasons relating to their higher carbon footprints and historical responsibility, as well as the fact that most behaviour change research is conducted in those countries. There is also increasing attention to the role of the richest – the 1 per cent – in driving climate change (Wiedmann et al., 2020) or what Kenner refers to as the 'polluter elite' (Kenner, 2019). Yet, as others note, rapidly industrialising countries are projected to contribute almost all the growth in carbon emissions. Increases in household consumption are driving much of that increase, as the expanding middle classes in China and India reach the per capita levels of the USA and EU, underscoring the importance of what has been referred to as 'lifestyle leapfrogging' (Schroeder & Anantharaman, 2017). Hence, as well as being attentive to the global and historical modes of exchange and extraction that sustain the carbon-intensive nature of richer peoples' lifestyles and make them possible, we also need to be attentive to the intra-societal dynamics of consumption and behaviour change.

This requires a re-framing of the behaviour change debate. Policies and initiatives must centre on what is to be gained from scaling sustainable behaviour change – rather than what is to be lost – in favour of revitalised notions of collective benefit, the common good, and reduced social and economic inequality. The neoliberal market model, aided and abetted by the advertising industry, has monopolised conceptions of the 'good life', making the articulation of alternative conceptions of the good life an urgent requirement in order to rapidly curtail consumption emissions (Soper, 2020). There is, after all, much to be gained from rising to this challenge, from cleaner air and more vibrant local economies, to enhanced leisure time (or 'time affluence' as Kasser and Sheldon 2009 put it) and improvements to well-being. Much existing research suggests it is possible to live a 'good life' within planetary boundaries (O'Neill et al., 2018; Hickel, 2019; Millward-Hopkins et al., 2020), and research on the 'spirit level' shows that beyond a certain level of income well-being indicators do not improve (Wilkinson & Pickett, 2009). Millward-Hopkins et al. (2020) also show how increases in carbon emissions are not coupled with increased life expectancy. In many cases, mitigating climate change and its impacts also need not be the central motivator for such societal shifts (Howell et al. 2016; Howell & Allen, 2017; RESET, 2020), and scaling behaviour change may in fact benefit from not always invoking climate concerns as its central driver.

Given the failure of the international community to bend the emissions curve over recent decades (Stokkard et al., 2021), a key neglected dimension of the debate is how behaviour change will be induced by the effects of global heating. Like it or not, the world is already committed to drastic change as a result of global heating (combined with other environmental and non-environmental threats). The impacts of climate change are already being felt today around the world by millions (Wallace-Wells, 2019). Our climatic future, where more frequent and severe impacts are now unavoidable, means that a certain degree of behaviour change will be inevitable, as humanity adapts to a warmer world. Behaviour change in this regard can be understood as a form of adaptation, where habitual behaviours, systems of provision, patterns of mobility, and consumption will shift to ensure resilience in the face of climate impacts (Semenza et al., 2011). This type of behaviour change is visible in altering food systems due to changing climates, crop failures and increased pests (Gomez-Zavaglia et al., 2020), as well as human migration in countries like Bangladesh (Bernzen et al., 2019) and regions like the Middle East and Central Asia (Piguet & Laczko, 2014). The terms of our adaptation, the depth of the changes and the pace at which they take place, and who bears the greatest costs of adjustment, are still very much up for contestation with important justice implications. As Greta Thunberg et al. note, 'we are inevitably going to have to fundamentally change, one way or another. The question is, will the changes be on our terms, or on nature's terms?' (2020). And if the 'our' refers to humanity as a whole, who precisely gets to set these terms?

Our Approach

To address the neglect of questions of politics, political economy, and governance in behaviour change and consumption debates, and limited attention to how to scale behaviour change, this Element builds an account that attends to issues of power, social justice, and governance, by exploring ideas about levers and tipping points and where future intervention points might lie in scaling change in line with the Paris Agreement and the SDGs. By investigating the types of politics and governance required to live well within planetary boundaries, and highlighting the ways in which responsibility and agency are unevenly distributed within and between societies, we seek to enhance our understanding of these key and often neglected aspects of earth system governance. The result is a more holistic understanding of behaviour, as just one node within an ecosystem of transformation that bridges the individual and systemic. Rather than generalising accounts of the need for behaviour change by all individuals, we emphasise the role of collective behaviour change among businesses, cities and states, and of particular social groups within societies, and within key high-impact behavioural 'hotspots'.

Our account is also more attentive to questions of governance and the processes of collective steering and learning necessary to facilitate large-scale change across a diversity of actors, sectors, and regions than the dominant emphasis on individuals and households in literature from psychology and economics, for example. As such, it adds a novel perspective to scholarship on multilevel governance by specifically relating it to behaviour change. It is also more historical in its approach, looking critically at the relevance of historical parallels regarding large-scale behaviour change and what might be learned and applied to the contemporary context, as well as locating contemporary inequities in consumption as part of historically uneven forms of extraction and exchange. The book draws on a report comprised of a detailed review of the relevant literature and practice, as well as in-depth interviews with 31 members of the *Cambridge Sustainability Commission on Scaling Behaviour Change*, made up of leading scholars and practitioners working on behaviour change, sustainable lifestyles, and climate policy (Newell et al., 2021).

We argue that behaviours are enabled and constrained, institutionalised and locked-in, reflecting and embodying power relations and social inequalities. That is why we need an account of behaviour change that centres on politics, governance, and social relations: because efforts to change behaviours need to be cognisant of and address these inequalities if they are not to further entrench them and be successful in scaling behaviour change; and power relations need to be disrupted so that control over production, technology, finance, institutions, legislation, and the provision of infrastructures by incumbent actors that benefit from unsustainable development, is reduced and relinquished.

We develop a more political account of behaviour change than those traditionally presented in the psychology and economic literature, for example, because any attempt to shift patterns of production and consumption will invite contentious politics and forms of resistance as it threatens elite control, ownership models, and concentrations of wealth. It also challenges deeply held values and societal givens about growth and materialism as the route to happiness, and, in so doing, affronts one of the assumptions underpinning contemporary capitalism: that consumption-induced growth is a prerequisite to societal well-being and human advancement. If we are to live differently, meet social needs and provide services in alternative ways, power and control over production, finance, and technology will need to be shared or, at the very least, opened-up to a broader range of actors invested in building a more sustainable future. Appreciating this, and grappling with it conceptually, requires an account grounded in political economy since behaviours are closely related to patterns of work and income, production and consumption, and articulations of social and environmental justice within and between societies. Approaches to scaling behaviour change that shy away from the need to re-wire the economy will fall short, in our view, of being effective and inclusive.

Though scholars of earth systems governance, and to a lesser extent global environmental politics (Maniates, 2001; Princen et al., 2002; Dauvergne, 2008), have often neglected the issue of sustainable consumption and the role of behaviour change in achieving it, the challenge of shifting patterns of production and consumption in a more sustainable direction is, at least in part, a question of governance. It involves goal setting, collective steering, management and coordination across multiple sites, domains and levels of governance (Biermann et al., 2017). This spans formal institutions, such as rulemaking and legislation, to hybrid and informal ones, incorporating new values, and the articulation and embedding of social norms. This comes close to the classic definitions of regime governance with their focus on 'norms, rules and decision-making procedures' (Krasner, 1983: 2). Given the range of actors involved in shaping dominant consumption patterns and that have a potentially key role in reconfiguring them: from cities to businesses, community organisations and social movements, our approach helps to build on scholarship on transnational climate change governance (Bulkeley et al., 2014; Hale, 2016) and the ways in which climate governance is accomplished in practice (Bulkeley, 2016). The emphasis we place here on networks and linkages across different sites of governance as part of an ecosystem of transformation also underscores the value of work on social network analysis and linkages in global environmental governance (Paterson et al., 2014; Betsill et al., 2015), as well as that which underscores the growing role of polycentric climate governance (Jordan et al., 2018).

Governance also speaks to the importance of citizen engagement for shaping the terms of future pathways and social acceptance of choices made given the uneven impacts and controversies about *how* and *by whom* limits are set, enforced, and policed. Innovative and robust governance systems are required to adjudicate and mediate between competing entitlements and claims on resources, and systems of service provision, now and in the future. Indeed, innovative governance systems are required to ensure that the structure, power dynamics, and patterns of behaviour that need to radically – and rapidly – change are not perpetuated. Since global budgets and limits need to be agreed between countries, there is a potential, yet currently under-developed, role for global governance in setting pathways and dealing with issues of responsibility, historical emissions, and justice.

The context in which governance systems are formed, and the spaces and arenas of politics within which discussions of sustainable behaviour change take place, are characterised by sharp inequalities. Social relations are important then because the gains, impacts of consumption and responsibility for it, are unevenly distributed across gender, race, and class, among other factors (Newell, 2005). We explore in this Element the key role of the polluter elite (Kenner, 2019) in debates about behaviour change, which highlights the centrality of class, power, and inequality. The role of the polluter elite extends beyond excessive consumption, high incomes, and carbon-intensive lifestyles to the wealth, investment decisions, lobbying efforts, and the myriad mechanisms and avenues that incumbents – who benefit greatly from the status quo – use to accommodate and resist calls for more systemic forms of change (Newell, 2018). When examining the polluter elite and behaviour change, we concur with Huber (2021) that 'we shouldn't just look at their consumption – we should ask *how they became rich in the first place*'. By centralising the notions of ownership and power, we use the polluter elite concept to combine the disproportionate impact of the most affluents' individual consumptive behaviours – owning multiple large homes, frequent air travel, and so on – with the underlying social relations of production and exploitation that stimulate consumption. Through this, we offer a more expansive understanding of responsibility that goes beyond the individual behaviours of the polluter elite to include their integral role in the formation and reproduction of capital. In other words, delivering behaviour change at the speed and scale now required not only means significant changes in the lifestyles of the most affluent, but also fundamental disruption and reconfiguration of the systems of ownership, production, and exploitation from which they profit.

This invites a more global and historical analysis of consumption since we need to decolonise this discussion and recognise how richer peoples' lifestyles rest on the continued extraction of wealth, resources, and the labour of poorer groups within their own societies and through trade and extractivism from other societies (Nikiforuk, 2012). There are historical and contemporary dimensions to this 'imperial mode of living' that must be accounted for (Brand & Wissen, 2018, 2021). For many wealthy people, primarily but not exclusively located in the Global North, these 'imperial lifestyles' of high consumption and luxury rely upon 'the unlimited appropriation of resources, a disproportionate claim to global and local ecosystems and sinks, and cheap labour from elsewhere' (Brand & Wissen, 2018: 152), often premised on racialised and gender understandings of whose labour and resources are valuable and whose are disposable. Bhattacharyya (2018: x) notes:

> racial capitalism . . . is intimately intertwined with the processes precipitating ecological crisis. The myth of expendability – of expendable peoples and expendable regions- haunts our time and is a key motor of the forms of capitalist development that operate on the assumption that some populations will never be included and will never reach viability or sustainability.

It is 'a mode of living that depends upon the worldwide exploitation of nature – and wage and non-wage labour – while simultaneously externalising the social and ecological consequences arising from it' (Brand & Wissen, 2021: 4), which it does across space and time. As we discuss later, entry points for challenging this system politically and culturally, rest on the ongoing political work that it requires to sustain the idea that this way of doing things is 'normal', 'natural' and 'inevitable' derived from projections of 'common sense' values and ways of living, even in the face of increasing evidence that it is none of those things. As scholarship in the Gramscian tradition shows (Newell, 2018; Brand & Wissen, 2021), these practices of domination and hegemony provoke resistance and counter-movements, the like of which we explore in Section 5.

The result of these dominant modes of extraction and exchange, however, is the material dispossession of others, predominantly in the Global South, as well as undermining the stability of the climate. As noted, any attempt to question or challenge the privilege intertwined with these imperial lifestyles will encounter fierce resistance because these issues are relational, especially in a context of limits and budgets: they are (often) zero sum. Not all social groups and sectors can continue to emit in the same way: some need to reduce much more to enable others to increase their emissions to meet basic needs and account for historical inequities, captured in the quote from Gandhi that the wealthy need to 'live simply so others may simply live'. This raises questions of justice, both its procedural and distributional elements, which run deeply through the politics of behaviour change. Transparent, trusted, and effective institutions will be needed to adjudicate between these competing claims, bringing us back to questions of governance.

This type of approach, we argue, is pertinent to the nature and scale of the challenge we now face, providing as it does the basis for a more political theory of change. Questions of the scale and speed of change now required cast serious doubt on the role of purely voluntary change, although it can play an important part. Infrastructures and service provision must change to meet societal needs for mobility, food, housing, heating and cooling, and so on, in more sustainable and affordable ways. This means that approaches to behaviour change need to be more nuanced: incorporating the interaction of individual *and* system change, and the ecosystems of transformation that provide entry points for accelerating change. They also need to be tailored to particular contexts where state capacity and willingness to intervene is uneven, the nature of civil societies diverge, and the organisation of the market takes various forms. Political science and political economy are well placed to help understand prospects of change across these different contexts by drawing attention to the structures that aggregate, mediate, and enable low-carbon behaviours.

This implies a more full-frontal critique of neoliberal approaches to behaviour change, but without indulging the comfortable default position of critics of neoliberalism that only system change will do and until it comes about, there is no role for individual agency and action. In turn, this implies a more sophisticated account of the multiple roles we play and the spaces we inhabit at home, at work, and as citizens in society. Intervention points and opportunities for leverage exist in multiple arenas and spaces. Our primary identities are often not as passive consumers or victims of industrialism, despite the neoliberal onslaught. This calls for a more nuanced, reflexive, and multidimensional account of behaviour change across actors and spaces of change from the home to the workplace, to the state and supranational bodies. It also emphasises the need to get to the roots of overconsumption through exploring work, income inequalities, and debt-fuelled consumption driven by an advertising industry that frames consumption as compensatory for excess work (Schor, 2011; Wilhite, 2016). Approaches that either seek to 'nudge' consumers and shift household behaviour in a vacuum (Thaler & Sunstein, 2009), or which adopt a 'plug and play' approach by substituting technology and services without shifting levels of consumption, production, or the power relations in which they are embedded (Newell & Martin, 2020), are unlikely to bring about the deeper, enduring change required.

The Structure of the Element

In the next section, we assess and review scholarship and strategies aimed at understanding the challenge of scaling, by first introducing the issues of planetary boundaries, social parameters, and political dimensions, which are integral to discussions about behaviour change. In Section 3, we then look at different ways of understanding behaviour change from disciplines as diverse as psychology, sociology, economics, and political economy. From there, in Section 4, we incorporate insights from science and technology studies to identify critical leverage and tipping points, before in the final section, proposing key future interventions for scaling behaviour change, where we employ the notion of an ecosystem of transformation as a heuristic for understanding and analysing the simultaneous reconfiguration of structures, systems, and actors to bring about the required social transformations for sustainability.

2 The Challenge of Scaling

There is significant contestation over the nature of the challenge of scaling behaviour change: whether incremental versus more transformative change is required, and whether *transitions within* or *transformations of* capitalism are necessary if questions of work, income, ownership, and consumerism are also a legitimate part of the conversation. Market liberal approaches emphasise technological innovation and metrics as a means to price environmental externalities without the need to reform the economy at large (Clapp & Dauvergne, 2011). More radical approaches suggest the need for fundamental change to the economic system itself (Trainer, 1995). Socialising the idea of limits means accepting the need to deal with vast inequalities, which poses deeply political questions. In the case of the former, they are an anathema to a growth-oriented capitalist economy (Hickel, 2019), while the latter are intrinsic to the way the current economy is organised (Piketty, 2014). There are also critical global governance challenges about how to allocate fair shares within and between societies, as proposed by some of the initiatives we discuss later. This allocation must acknowledge the fact that for large segments of humanity, predominantly in the Global South, but also within richer nations in the Global North, an increase in consumption is necessary to raise the standard of living and improve human well-being, such as through the provision of housing, healthcare, and food. In other words, it is the inequality between patterns of over and under-consumption in the economy that needs to be addressed.

Defining Parameters

There is increasing emphasis on the inevitability of targets regarding *what* has to be reduced by *when*, if we want to remain within ecological limits (Lorek & Fuchs, 2013). However, limits are highly controversial and difficult to enforce in a neoliberal context due to ideological commitments to notions of consumer sovereignty, freedom of choice, and the rejection of the notion of either limits or sufficiency. This may explain the appeal of the idea of 'plentitude', which we discuss later (Schor, 2011): liberating time and freedom for creative and civic expression in return for constraints on excessive consumption and income. Some advocates of de-growth are also critical of the notion of limits because 'the notion of limits puts us on the wrong foot from the start. It presupposes that nature is something "out there", separate from us, like a stern authority hemming us in. This kind of thinking emerges from the very dualist ontology that got us into trouble in the first place' (Hickel, 2020: 34), arguing instead for 'interconnectedness': a deeper value shift in our relationship to nature.

Unsurprisingly, this ambivalence is also reflected in the collective reluctance among political leaders to convincingly confront the need for limits. In this vacuum interesting things are nevertheless happening. Amsterdam's City Doughnut initiative, which 'downscales' the concept of a 'global doughnut', strives to create a circular economy, operating in the space between its social foundations and ecological ceilings (Raworth et al., 2020, also see Table 1). We also note later the importance of governance innovations such as citizen's assemblies to drive climate action from below, while also challenging

Table 1 Defining fair shares for sustainability[1]

Approach	Means	Level
Contraction and Convergence[2]	Per capita carbon entitlements.	Globally agreed
Greenhouse Development Rights framework[3]	Calculation of responsibility and capacity beyond a development threshold.	Globally agreed
Individual carbon allowances/rations derived from global carbon budgets[4]	Per capita entitlements. A carbon ration operates as a simple allowance (in kilos of carbon), paid into a digital ration account to citizens.	Globally agreed, nationally implemented
Carbon fee and dividend[5]	Enforced through an initial fee of $15/metric tonne on the CO_2 equivalent emissions of fossil fuels. The proposal is that this would rise by $10/metric tonne each year. 100 per cent of the net fees from	Globally and nationally

---

[1] For a useful review of many of these approaches, see van den Berg et al. (2020).
[2] http://gci.org.uk/   [3] http://gdrights.org/about/
[4] https://carbonrationing.org/support-for-total-carbon-rationing/
[5] https://citizensclimatelobby.org/basics-carbon-fee-dividend/

Table 1 (cont.)

Approach	Means	Level
	the carbon fee would then be held in a Carbon Fees Trust fund and returned directly to households as a monthly dividend.[6] A border tax adjustment to stop business relocation.	
Sustainable Consumption Corridors (Di Guilio & Fuchs, 2014; Fuchs et al., 2021)	Defining upper and lower limits or thresholds of consumption.	Corridors agreed and implemented in local and national contexts, but with consideration of global conditions and the needs of future generations
Doughnut Economics[7]	Outer limits set by planetary boundaries. Inner floor set by basic social needs.	National, city level
Ecological footprint analysis[8]	Compares a population's demand on productive ecosystems with biocapacity (the ability of those ecosystems to keep up with this demand).[9]	National, city or individual

6 https://citizensclimatelobby.org/basics-carbon-fee-dividend/
7 www.kateraworth.com/doughnut/
8 www.footprintnetwork.org/our-work/ecological-footprint/
9 www.footprintnetwork.org/our-work/ecological-footprint/

incumbent control of the conversations around what are deemed 'plausible' and 'realistic' responses to climate crisis.

A key challenge is how to socialise the idea that radical shifts in production and consumption, including behaviour change, are required. The 'Overton window' is often referred to this context and describes the six stages that ideas pass through on the path from being politically marginal to becoming actual policy implemented in the real world: 1. Unthinkable, 2. Radical, 3. Acceptable, 4. Sensible, 5. Popular, 6. Policy. A key question then is what this would look like for a strong sustainable consumption agenda: for proposals currently deemed too radical and unthinkable to become accepted policies enjoying popular support, ones which emphasise the need for a reduction in overall resource consumption, instead of looking at relative reductions in individual consumption (Fuchs & Lorek, 2005; Lorek & Fuchs, 2013; Anantharaman, 2018). This approach is contrasted with a weak sustainable consumption approach that focuses on efficiency gains in existing patterns of consumption through technological innovations and small-scale behaviour change.

One Planet Living: Ecological Boundaries and Limits to Growth

Part of re-framing this debate means moving from *efficiency* to *sufficiency* in order to shift the debate on limits and prosperity. To achieve the goals of the Paris Agreement, countries need to look beyond efficiency improvements and emissions intensity targets towards absolute reductions in energy consumption, as well as address the drivers of overconsumption more broadly. Discussing innovations in residential energy use, Spangenberg and Lorek (2019: 287) suggest that 'to be effective, efficiency measures have to be embedded in a concept of sufficiency which strives for limits and absolute reduction of energy consumption'. This reflects the fact that while energy efficiency increased significantly across OECD countries, total energy consumption only decreased marginally because of the existence of rebound effects whereby money saved from efficiencies gets spent on further energy consumption (Sorrell et al., 2009).

A move towards sufficiency recognises that we need to set upper limits on consumption either through personal carbon budgets, rationing measures, or sustainable consumption corridors. Such a shift would fundamentally question cultural and social values around what it means to live a 'good life'. In other words, what provision of services and level of consumption is *sufficient* for a good life (Princen, 2005)? There is growing interest in well-being, sustainable prosperity (Jackson et al., 2016), prosperity without growth (Jackson, 2011), post-growth (Jackson, 2021), alternative hedonism (Soper, 2020), and the idea of 'plentitude' (Schor, 2011). De-growth, meanwhile, also signifies 'a desired direction, one in which societies will use fewer natural resources and will organize and live differently than today. Sharing, simplicity, conviviality, care, and the commons are primary signifiers of what this society might look like' (D'Alisa et al., 2015: 3). Such a shift also implies new indicators of progress. These include happiness indicators such as Gross National Happiness as adopted by Bhutan or the Happy Planet Index developed by the New Economics Foundation to 'measure what matters: sustainable wellbeing for all', which assesses nations according to their ability to support 'long, happy, sustainable lives' (NEF, 2016). There are also calls for what Soper labels 'alternative structures of satisfactions' (2020: 4) that consider the different social and cultural contexts behaviours take place within, rather than top-down prescriptions of what constitutes basic or universal needs. What follows is social innovation to drive shifts in business practice, technology development, and innovation to support sustainable lifestyles (Westley et al., 2011; Hiteva & Sovacool, 2017).

Cultures of consumption (Dauvergne, 2008) are critical here alongside the dominant focus on productionist drivers of technology, innovation, and finance and their role in meeting rising demand. Managing demand and addressing consumption, rather than just varying supply, is key: tackling the problem with both arms of the scissors. For example, how far should we invest in new supply as opposed to reduce demand? Retrofitting existing buildings is essential as 90 per cent of buildings today will still be operational in 2050. Retrofitting and demand reduction is much more cost-effective, but the debate is all about expanding supply (Boardman, 2010). Discussions around food and energy futures tend to forecast and then presume ever-increasing demand and consumption, as if it is necessary to support societal well-being. The only remaining choices are, therefore, which technologies and policies meet that growth, regardless of whether that growth is sustainable, whether demand can be reduced, or whether efficiency and conservation measures can reduce waste. Many of these assumptions are baked into even the most ambitious integrated assessment model (IAM) mitigation scenarios set out in the IPCC's SR1.5 all of which assume continued growth in GDP, questionable amounts of CDR, and unprecedented technological innovation (Kuhnhenn, 2018). On this basis, Keyßer and Lenzen (2021) call for new mitigation pathways and IAMs that directly engage with de-growth scenarios in order to reduce the current overreliance on technology-driven pathways.

Table 1 summarises various attempts to define the parameters of consumption.

Taking the analysis down a level, some scholars look at sectoral parameters for consumption in order to assess their compatibility within global ecological limits. Moore (2015), for example, develops consumption benchmarks in the domains of food, buildings, consumables, transportation, and water by combining ecological footprint analysis with 'lifestyle archetypes'. She explores the sorts of transformative changes that would be needed for the per capita consumption patterns of average global urban dwellers to achieve ecological sustainability including: a 73 per cent reduction in household energy use, a 96 per cent reduction in motor vehicle ownership, a 78 per cent reduction in per capita vehicle kilometres travelled, and a 79 per cent reduction in air kilometres travelled (Moore, 2015: 4747). Her work clearly underscores that in a world where there is still no clear substitution for certain activities, the goal must be *absolute* and not just *relative* reductions.

Meanwhile, the Ecological Footprint concept compares a population's demand on productive ecosystems (its footprint) – with the ability of those ecosystems to keep up with this demand (biocapacity). The Global Footprint Network's 'National Footprint Accounts' tracks the footprints of countries by measuring the area of cropland, grazing land, forest, and fisheries required to produce the food, fibre, and timber resources being consumed and to absorb the CO_2 waste emitted when burning fossil fuels.[2] Ecological Footprint studies reveal that currently the 'world is in ecological overshoot by as much as 50 percent' (Rees & Moore, 2013: 42). There is significant scepticism, nevertheless, about the use of some types of footprint tools amid the proliferation of apps and tools – with increasingly pervasive data harvesting capabilities – to measure peoples' carbon use (and monitor their consumption habits), especially when supported by industry actors such as oil companies. Here there is a valid concern about such tools serving as a diversionary tactic to shift attention away from their own responsibility to act, instead placing the onus to change – as well as the blame for emissions – on individual consumers (Supran & Osreskes, 2021). And more insidious still, they enable corporations to gain access to data about individuals' consumption preferences in order to better target their products to them.

Social Dimensions: Just Transitions

Any discussion of limits invites a conversation about distribution within those limits. This is based on an underlying assumption that the changes required to get the world onto a 1.5-degree pathway should not be shouldered equally by all in society. As Figure 1 illustrates, the average per capita emissions share of CO_2

---

[2] www.footprintnetwork.org/2016/03/08/national-footprint-accounts/

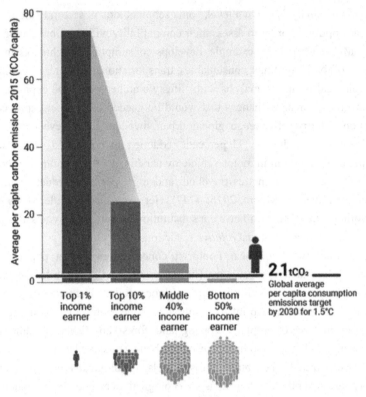

Figure 1 Per capita and absolute CO_2 consumption emissions by four global
income groups in 2015
Source: *UNEP Emissions Gap Report 2020*

varies strikingly between income groups. Considerable effort is required to
ensure the socially differentiated drivers and contexts of consumption are
addressed seriously to avoid individualising responsibility or saddling poorer
groups with a disproportionate burden to act. Kevin Anderson (2018) has
shown, for example, that if the richest 10 per cent of society were to bring
their emissions in line with the level of the average European, and the remaining
90 per cent of humanity made no adjustments to their lifestyles, then global
emissions would drop by one-third within a couple of years.

It is a small percentage of humanity that needs to make the greatest transformations in their lifestyle – a fact that is all too often overlooked in public
debate around sustainable behaviour change. Key to the successful design and
social acceptance of any scheme to set and enforce limits and constraints on
consumption, also known as 'shrink and share' schemes, therefore, is equitable
allocation. Rees and Moore (2013) consider 1.7 gha/per capita to be each
person's equitable or 'fair Earth-share' of global biocapacity. Currently, more

than half the world's population lives at or below a fair Earth-share. Most of those people are based in Latin America, Asia, and Africa (2013: 42).

Political Dimensions

The process for agreeing on those limits and determining the means by which they should be achieved raises a series of complex, ultimately political, issues about which there has to be a public discussion (Fuchs et al., 2021). Public deliberation, culminating in political demands and execution, needs to determine minimum socially acceptable limits, which together with an understanding of planetary boundaries, translate into maximum consumption limits, if all individuals living now and in the future are to have the opportunity to achieve the minimum levels of consumption. In this scenario, the minimum is defined by what constitutes a good life, and the good life is defined by being able to satisfy needs (as opposed to wants). This relates closely to the idea of doughnut economics: a safe operating space for humanity whereby key developmental needs are met within ecological planetary boundaries (Raworth, 2017).

Current and historical inequalities within and across societies need to be addressed by 'shrink and share' schemes that limit and redistribute future entitlements to both production and consumption (see Table 1). This is the premise of proposals for *'contraction and convergence'* (towards an agreed per capita carbon entitlement), for example, which demand larger and nearer term reductions from richer countries that have over-used carbon space, and smaller and slower reductions from poorer countries that have pressing development needs to meet and who have contributed far less to the problem of global heating thus far (GCI, 2018), as well as the *Greenhouse Development Rights* framework that only applies to citizens above a specific development threshold and only then on the basis of a calculation of responsibility and capacity to act (GDR, 2018). Employing these criteria, the *Civil Society Equity Review* (2018) concludes that the most equitable mitigation framework would see the richest 10 per cent globally take responsibility for 87 per cent of the total emissions cuts needed, while the poorest 50 per cent are not yet required to cut emissions at all. Underscoring this analysis, SEI and Oxfam have produced a database that covers 117 countries, around 90 per cent of the world's population, and global carbon emissions across the 1990–2015 period. They conclude:

> The disproportionate impact of the world's richest people is unmistakable –
> nearly half of the total growth in absolute emissions was due to the richest
> 10 per cent (the top two ventiles), with the richest 5 per cent alone contribut-
> ing over a third (37%). The remaining half was due almost entirely to the
> contribution of the middle 40% of the global income distribution (the next

eight ventiles). The impact of the poorest half (the bottom ten ventiles) of the world's population was practically negligible (Kartha et al., 2020: 7).

It is important to keep in mind, however, that there is critical scope to avoid 'carbon lock-in' (Unruh, 2000) through the provision of services and choice architectures for poorer communities and thus to enable a degree of 'lifestyle leapfrogging' (Schroeder & Anantharaman, 2017).

There is, therefore, a clear and obvious need to tackle uneven consumption within countries. Across Europe, analysis reveals that the emission reductions achieved since 1990 have predominantly come from lifestyle changes and the reduced consumption of lower- and middle-income EU citizens, while the total emissions of the richest 10 per cent have grown. Over the period of 1990 to 2015, the richest 10 per cent of EU citizens were responsible for 27 per cent of the EU's total cumulative emissions – the same amount of emissions as the poorest half of the EU population combined (Gore & Alestig, 2020). We can see then the divergent nature of consumption among different income groups, with the richest sections of society actually increasing their consumption-related emissions, while the sharp contractions in emissions have taken place among the middle- and lower-income groups. Gore and Alestig (2020) note that between 1990 and 2015, the poorest 50 per cent of the EU population's consumption emissions fell by 24 per cent and emissions from the 40 per cent of 'middle income' Europeans fell by 13 per cent, respectively. Emissions from the most affluent 10 per cent of European citizens, however, grew by 3 per cent and those from the wealthiest 1 per cent – the super-rich – rose by 5 per cent. These figures clearly show the need for a differentiated approach to behaviour change, as well as how the responsibility for emission reductions is not shared equally across society. For example, to meet a 1.5-degree consistent emissions pathway by 2030, the richest 1 per cent of humanity needs to reduce their emissions by a factor of *at least* 30, while the poorest 50 per cent could increase their emissions by around three times the current level (Gore & Alestig, 2020).

How reductions are made needs to be attentive to inequalities within societies to ensure extra burdens are not merely passed onto poorer and excluded groups, and those already vulnerable to the impacts of climate change. Anantharaman (2014) highlights the invisible and implied labour behind the performance of sustainable lifestyles: the informal and gendered economies that, in some contexts at least, involve domestic staff, waste pickers, and fleets of informal construction workers (for insulation, solar photovoltaic (PV) installation, etc.). Levels of inequality within society are important here not only in terms of responsibility, or because they determine who bears the cost of action, but because they drive competitive consumption (Schor, 2015). As Danny

Dorling (2017) highlights, 'in more unequal societies, there is a proliferation of products that are designed not to last, so as to allow greater profits to be made. Producing endless must-have new versions exploits the higher levels of emotional insecurity that living with great inequality generates'. Soper (2020: 64) puts it more bluntly still, noting that 'people are exhorted to define and value themselves in terms of what they can afford to acquire even if this means borrowing to do so'.

Addressing these injustices also speaks to the need to decolonise the sustainable living debate. As research on ecologically uneven exchange and global environmental justice (Roberts & Parks, 2008; Sikor & Newell, 2014; Brand & Wissen, 2021) clearly shows, the unsustainable consumption by elites the world over is only possible because of racialised, gendered, and class-based modes of extraction and appropriation organised around 'cheapness' (Patel & Moore, 2018), constituted historically, but ever present today in the way the social and environmental costs and benefits of consumption and production are unevenly distributed within and between societies. The need to address these issues is underscored by the above-mentioned analysis of historical inequities, carbon debts, and the overuse of resources by polluter elites that must underpin debates around fair shares, carbon budgets, or rationing proposals.

By being conscious of economic and social injustices, strategies can be effective at empowering citizens and capturing a variety of co-benefits with important implications for scalability. Perkins (2019) suggests that addressing economic injustices is a *precondition* for participatory governance and equitable solutions, as the ubiquity of economic injustices actively reduces the *political space* for climate action. Directly addressing economic injustices could therefore create the (pre)conditions and space for scaling sustainable behaviour change. There are also vital racial, class, and gender dimensions to access and responsibility that all interventions and strategies must be conscious of and explicitly address the intersectionalities between them (Johnson et al., 2020). For example, patterns of energy access, access to low-carbon technologies, and vulnerability to price rises during transitions are all heavily racialised (Newell, 2020), gendered, and manifest in other social inequalities (Hooper et al., 2021).

There has been renewed interest in a universal basic income (UBI) and some experimentation with this in parts of Europe, as one way to tackle some of these inequalities. For example, in Grande-Synthe, on the outskirts of Dunkirk in France, a guaranteed social minimum (MSG) has been tested since April 2019. Forty per cent of the 1.2 million Euros budgeted to fund the scheme comes from the savings made by replacing bulbs in public lighting with LEDs. Interest in UBI builds on long-standing calls from feminists for paid care work or 'care work as commons'.[3] However, there are emerging concerns that a UBI may not enable the reductions in consumption-related emissions needed to align with a 1.5-degree target (Lawhon & McCreary, 2020). One study in Finland found that the average annual carbon footprint at the UBI level – the lowest income decile – was around 4.8 tCO2 equivalent (Kalaniemi et al., 2020). This is substantially lower than the average carbon footprint in Finland of 9.4 tCO2 equivalent, but still far from compatible with a 1.5-degree lifestyle (Akenji et al., 2019). While more research is required in this area, initial findings suggest that to be an effective mitigation tool, a UBI that seeks to address economic injustices must be combined with broader shifts in values, behaviours, and the provision of services and infrastructures.

What scholarship also points to is the need to focus on particularly carbon-intensive behaviours, or what are referred to as hotspots. The *1.5-Degree Lifestyles* report (Akenji et al., 2019) found that just three domains (nutrition, housing, and mobility) have the largest impact, amounting to approximately 75 per cent of total lifestyle carbon footprint. If measures in each of these areas were to be fully implemented, they could reduce the footprint of each hotspot domain by anything from a few hundred kilograms to over a tonne annually (Akenji et al., 2019: vi). Ivanova et al. (2020) find overall that for many of these measures, 'the top ten consumption options together yield an average mitigation potential of 9.2 tCO2eq/cap, indicating substantial contributions towards achieving the 1.5∘C–2∘C target, particularly in high-income context' (2020: 1).[4] Many authors are at pains to point out, however, that any such gains are contingent on changes across society and the economy. As the *1.5-Degree Lifestyles* report makes clear: 'The required levels of reductions, exceeding 90 per cent based on current lifestyle carbon footprints, imply a *radical rethink of sustainability governance* and the need for new business models to shift the paradigms on which we base infrastructure, economies and consumer lifestyles' (Akenji et al., 2019: 5; emphasis added).

Questions of speed, urgency, and the scale of the challenge also change the politics of behaviour change. As noted in Section 1, incremental, individual-level change is no longer enough (if they ever were). But it also raises issues of 'post-politics' (Swyngedouw, 2010), and how emphasis on urgency is used to rule out more structural and systemic forms of change on the basis that we don't have time to bring them about. This is sometimes in tension with the need to ensure that transformations are just, equitable, intergenerationally fair, and institutionally sustainable. Fostering more long-term thinking is required to

---

[3] https://www.degrowth.info/blog/carework-as-commons-towards-a-feminist-degrowth-agenda
[4] For more on David Fleming's proposal see https://www.flemingpolicycentre.org.uk/faqs/

escape the 'tyranny of the now' – which is also the driver for much consumption in affluent societies.

By means of bringing together the key threads outlined in this section, we draw on a threefold conceptualisation of scaling (Newell et al., 2021a). First, we refer to the dominant, rational understanding of behaviour change – associated with mainstreaming, efficiency gains, 'nudges', and behavioural contagion – as *'shallow'* scaling. Second, as an alternative, ideal-type pathway, we highlight the urgent need for *'deep'* scaling, whereby behaviour change is viewed as an orchestrated social transformation or paradigm shift, occurring when sustainable values and norms become deliberately, culturally and institutionally embedded. Such a transition calls for a diversity of means, adapted to different social, cultural, political, and economic contexts, and for ends to be specified in terms of limits and timeframes. Finally, we offer a third conceptual space, which we term *'spiral'* scaling, inspired by O'Brien et al.'s (2013: 6) 'axial revolution' for transforming education and capacity-building for global sustainability. This depicts the transformation from 'shallow' to 'deep' scaling as a dynamic sequence of learning-loop feedbacks, between individuals, society, institutions and infrastructures, towards 'strong' sustainability and sufficiency. As such, it ultimately represents the messy space where much of the transition to sustainable behaviour and systems change will ultimately play out. As noted in Section 1, different disciplines inform our understanding of how to scale behaviour change, employing different theories of change and methodological and epistemological starting points with different implications for politics and policy with regard to what is deemed 'possible'. We proceed by introducing and analysing the contributions to the behaviour change debate of four key disciplines in the next section, before presenting our own prescriptions for future interventions in Section 5.

3 Understanding Behaviour Change

In this section we develop the argument that scaling behaviour change means using multiple intervention points within an ecosystem of transformation. Whereas existing theories and approaches to behaviour change focus on one part of that ecosystem (values, behaviours, structures, institutions), our argument is that they should not be thought of in opposition to one another, but as part of a mutually reinforcing guide to change that can be adapted to different contexts and opportunities.

We explore the limits of dominant, individualist approaches to scaling behaviour change, and demonstrate why they are ineffective as stand-alone responses in the face of the structural change required due to: a tendency to fall into the 'scalar' trap, to be techno-centric in their approach, and to present an undifferentiated account of agency and responsibility for behaviour change. We also note the politics of why these approaches are favoured: because they usually fail to challenge the status quo or existing power structures and individualise responsibility and agency through atomisation. Towards this end, we suggest that accounts of individual change afford useful insights and highlight the importance of personal change and value shifts, but that more social and sociological accounts of practice and culturing change, as well as political economy's emphasis on the drivers of overconsumption, afford important traction in identifying and leveraging points of intervention, which we return to in the final section of this Element.

So, what insights can we glean from the existing disciplinary research on how best to scale behaviour change? While many academics may agree to disagree over the means and merits of sustainable behaviour change strategies to achieve 1.5°C lifestyles, there is broad consensus that different theoretical approaches can help us to identify and tackle different pieces of the puzzle. Here we principally draw on four disciplinary perspectives. The first two, *'nudge'* theory and *psychological* approaches, take the individual as the basis for analysis and have tended to dominate contemporary behaviour change discourses and policies to date. As they see agency as primary, they tend to be more optimistic about prospects for behaviour change. The second pair, *sociology* and practice theories, and *political economy*, see *systems* as being critical contexts within which individuals operate, and therefore behaviour is understood to be driven and circumscribed by social, political, and physical structures, which are slower to evolve, harder to disrupt, and reproduce uneven dynamics of power across race, gender, and class. Since we argue that individual *and* system change are required, we make the case for moving forward by combining these insights.

'Nudge' Theory

The concept of 'nudge' comes from the behavioural economics tradition that believes people can be coaxed into making 'better choices' using the power of suggestion and positive reinforcement, without the need to change the alternatives available to them (Nature Human Behaviour, 2020). As popularised by Thaler and Sunstein (2009: 6), a nudge is defined as, 'any aspect of the choice architecture that alters people's behaviour in a predictable way without forbidding any options or significantly changing their economic incentives'. By altering the choice architecture, therefore, optimal outcomes (in this case more sustainable behaviours) become more predictable, without infringing on one's individual liberty through manipulative means. Lehner et al. (2016) suggest that nudge interventions make use of four tools to alter the choice architecture: simplification and framing of information, which is the most commonly utilised for sustainability purposes (Thøgersen & Schrader, 2012); adjustments to the physical environment; changing default policies (Momsen & Stoerk, 2014) (around green electricity, for example), and the use of social norms, such as initiatives that gamify recycling through neighbourly competition (John et al., 2013). Nudge theory has come in for criticism for being 'neoliberal' or using 'soft paternalism' (Jones et al., 2011), due to its emphasis on the individualisation of responsibility, entrenching the idea that economic rationality is the sole driver for decision-making (Berg & Gigerenzer, 2010), as well as potentially being undemocratic (Goodwin, 2012).

Although evidence shows that nudging individuals in the right direction can achieve a degree of success in changing behaviour (Shepherd et al., 2014), its reach is generally confined to specific, simple and narrow contexts (Nisa et al., 2019), and as such, its capacity to affect behaviour change to date has been notoriously limited (Nature Human Behaviour, 2020). This is partly because nudge efforts are vulnerable to 'rebound' effects (Sorrell et al., 2009). For example, buying a more fuel-efficient or hybrid car might cause a driver to make longer or more frequent journeys ('direct' rebounds) or spend the money saved on additional goods and services leading to further energy and resource use ('indirect' and 'time-use' rebounds). Some estimate that direct rebounds alone can be in the order of 30 per cent (Sorrell et al., 2009).

Another significant reason why nudge on its own may be destined to fail in certain circumstances is that it is poorly equipped to address countervailing psychological and systemic influences (Burningham & Venn, 2017). Supporters of nudge would, of course, argue that failing to engage with attitudes, values, and beliefs does not necessarily reduce the ability to facilitate behaviour change towards more socially or economically optimal outcomes. As Lehner et al. suggest 'in order to change behaviour we do not always need to change minds' (2016: 14). Nudge theorists would also highlight the relative affordability of interventions and their political palatability, as they are often seen as less controversial than restrictive and coercive policy measures (Avineri & Goodwin, 2010). Nudge interventions' effectiveness depends on their acceptance by the public, which is easier to gain if there is some sort of consensus around the 'ends' of the nudge (Lehner et al., 2016). As public concern around climate change continues to grow in many nations, there is scope for nudge interventions supportive of low-carbon behaviours. However, given that we are seeking to urgently change embedded patterns across a range of behaviours (and not just instigate individual actions), it seems inevitable that we will need to look beyond nudge approaches. As Dolan et al. conclude, 'the best interventions will certainly be those that seek to change minds alongside changing contexts' (2012: 274).

Psychological Approaches

Taking a more cognitive approach to behaviour, social, and environmental psychology essentially see values (personal, guiding principles) and identity (how people define themselves) as the 'building blocks of public engagement' (McLoughlin et al., 2019: 16). Whereas public opinion and attitudes can shift, surge, and wane, it is argued that values and identity tend to be more stable and consistent across contexts, which can be helpful in framing communications and targeting interventions to promote conscious change and embed low-carbon lifestyles – rather than simply triggering a collection of disparate pro-climate actions (Nash et al., 2017).

Psychological studies in the field of climate change have been helpful in identifying targets and exploring the potential for behavioural change through specific interventions to improve the uptake of high climate-impact actions (Nielsen et al., 2020: 25), often by highlighting individual and social barriers and constraints (information, financial, confidence, time, mobility, expertise), and indicating how they can be overcome (Lorenzoni et al., 2007; Dietz et al., 2009). They have also contributed to our understandings of positive 'spill-over' effects (also referred to as 'catalyst' or 'wedge' behaviours) (DEFRA, 2008: 22). These operate like the first rung on a ladder of engagement by assuming that one relatively simple, targeted eco-behaviour can lead to another (e.g. recycling at home, leading to recycling at work), which may, in principle, result in more radical structural changes over time, especially if behaviour spills over into social and political realms (Thøgersen & Noblet, 2012). This effect may further be enhanced if motivations and convictions are targeted (Barr et al., 2010, Thøgersen, 1999), which can mitigate to a degree against negative spillovers (Bolderdijk et al., 2013), as well as associated 'moral licensing', whereby one environmentally 'virtuous' action (such as reusing or recycling plastic) is used to justify other unsustainable behaviours (such as buying more plastic) (Zhong et al., 2010). This evidence of conflicting motivations, values, and identities, often pulling in different directions, also demonstrates that presenting the co-benefits of low-carbon actions can be an effective way of appealing to diverse motivations across the value spectrum. Indeed, it may go some way towards mitigating against the attitude-behaviour and intention-action gaps that have long confounded academics, policymakers, NGOs, and green marketeers, whereby individuals report eco-consciousness, but fail to act correspondingly

(Kollmuss & Agyeman, 2002; White et al., 2019a, b). Encouragingly, Bain et al. (2016: 1) found that by presenting the co-benefits of 'development' (understood here as 'economic and scientific advancement') and 'benevolence' ('a more moral and caring community') in promoting actions to combat climate change, people across 24 countries were motivated to engage in private, public, and financial activities to a similar degree, whether or not they were convinced about the validity or importance of climate change itself (Bain et al., 2016: 1).

Priming also has the potential to trigger environmentally conscious behaviour, by activating intrinsic values at the point of choice, around the purchase of organic food, for example (Thøgersen & Alfinito, 2020). Interestingly from the point of view of governance, experiments have also found that invoking 'citizenship' rather than consumerism, led to decreased orientations towards materialistic concerns, while exposure to consumerist cues was associated with reduced interest in social involvement, greater competitiveness, and lower feelings of responsibility (Bauer et al., 2012). As Kasser points out, 'all of us have materialistic tendencies ... researchers need to ask not only, "Who is materialistic?" but also "*When* are people materialistic?"' (2016: 506, emphasis added). For this reason, understanding that people are conflicted and fallible, and reminding them of how their actions relate to their values, clearly has a part to play in bringing about sustainable behaviour change, especially given that materialistic priming – via marketing, sponsorship, and advertising campaigns – remains ubiquitous in most societies.

Just as behavioural psychology has extensively informed communication and marketing strategies (UNEP, 2005), effective framing, messaging and modelling will be key to delivering sustainable behaviour change at scale. Lessons we can draw are, first, that the source of the message is as important as its content because information will be filtered by political and social allegiances (White et al., 2019b). When people are actively deliberating a choice and engaging in decision-making, they seek information from sources they trust, that is, those they share common values with (friends, family, neighbours) or from independent/formal sources they consider to be objective and competent (e.g. health professionals, NGOs, teachers, scientists). Given that trust and communication are both dynamic, there is scope for trust to be built, as well as eroded, by opinion leaders, communicators, and policy actors (Sleeth-Keppler et al., 2017), which can happen particularly rapidly when social media channels are employed, as we have seen during the COVID-19 pandemic.

Modelling can also be influential, particularly from socially relevant, aspirational figures, who can demonstrate, and help rewrite what is understood to be 'the done thing' (e.g. celebrities, entertainers, social media influencers, sports personalities, religious leaders) (Gächter & Renner, 2018). Finally, proximity to others can also lead to scaling by social contagion, as has been found to be the case in the uptake of solar panels and electric vehicles in local neighbourhoods (Bollinger & Gillingham, 2012; Frank, 2020). This ties in with related research proposing the use of more empowering cues, such as telling a positive story, projecting self-efficacy, and highlighting co-benefits – such as health, well-being, and community cohesion (McLoughlin et al., 2019). In the policy sphere, this also suggests the need for an integrated approach to generate maximum impact (Spence & Pigeon, 2009: 13).

A further – and potentially significant – route to maximising the reach of behaviour change stems from the understanding that individuals not only hold multiple values simultaneously, but also assume various roles and operate across numerous spheres of influence. By thinking of behaviour in these expansive terms, the impact of individual agency can be extended well beyond the sum of a person's discrete actions, and amplified across families, friendship circles, workplaces, social and religious groups, schools and learning institutions, leisure and sports clubs, NGOs, corporations, and other organisations and networks (Tosun & Schoenefeld, 2016). The Sitra report (2020) demonstrates this potential, by calculating not only the carbon footprints of fictional individuals based on their lifestyle-archetype profiles, but also describes and quantifies the spillovers corresponding to their pro-eco behaviours in terms of emissions saved, which they call, 'carbon handprints'. It is more evident still, as we argue in this Element, in the case of the 'polluter elite'. For example, in their study of the role of 'high-socioeconomic-status people' in reducing GHG emissions, Nielsen et al. (2021) identify five roles where they have a disproportionate capacity to apply influence – as consumers, investors, role models, organisational participants, and citizens. They explain,

> Whether people lobby directly or through their roles in private or non-profit organizations, the greatest influence comes from small numbers of highly influential people .... For example, two fossil fuel billionaires, acting over decades, had a profound influence in shifting the policy discourse in the United States to the right, including the ascendency of politicians favouring low taxes, opposed to environmental protection and climate action, and mistrustful of government overall. (Nielsen et al., 2021: 4)

Others, from a psychoanalytical and psychosocial persuasion, highlight the conflicted, affective, and defensive nature of the human mind, and believe that too narrow a focus on values often fails to acknowledge the internal struggles and barriers people face to live by their values and reconcile the contradictions of sustainable living in today's complex world (Lertzman, 2014). They point out that climate anxiety can cause overwhelm, denial and disavowal, and lead to anger, paralysis, and the suspension of reality, which prevents people from acting creatively and engaging in problem-solving: something we have seen all too clearly in public debates about climate change and sustainability. As Adams (2013: 52) explains: 'Despite increased knowledge, the populaces of wealthy nations appear to be outwardly ignoring such risks, continuing their consumption patterns unabated, and failing to mount a significant public response.' In order to break this impasse, and address the 'social organisation of denial' (Adams, 2013), psychoanalysts advocate safe spaces to talk about lifestyle, and believe that more profound opportunities for engagement in sustainable behaviour change via dialogue and connection, and creating inclusive and dynamic spaces to hold difficult conversations, will be key. This raises challenges of collective psychology: a broader cultural developmental process. It is at this deeper level that it is perhaps hardest to engage and change, but where the most profound and lasting change can come: via shifts in values and worldviews.

Sociology and Social Practice

Having begun with an analysis of behavioural approaches, associated with 'methodological individualism', we move on to explore how systemic theories understand and elucidate behaviour change. We turn first to sociological approaches, which highlight the need to place individual behaviours within a wider social context to help identify the enabling conditions for achieving sustainable lifestyles.

Sociologists argue that by focussing too much on individuals, behavioural models fail to sufficiently account for complex social and cultural processes (Stephenson et al., 2010; Sovacool & Griffiths, 2020), as well as physical and economic 'lock-in' (Unruh, 2000; Sanne, 2002). Instead, they believe social and physical structures are woven together into webs of understandings, strongly derived (and perpetuated) by culture, and co-determined by norms, objects, symbols, identities, and practices, which give meaning to life (Jackson, 2006). As Warde (2014: 284) explains: 'Against the model of the sovereign consumer, practice theories emphasise routine over actions, flow and sequence over discrete acts, dispositions over decisions, and practical consciousness over deliberation.' In relation to sustainable lifestyles, behavioural approaches also neglect what Shove (2003) calls the 'social organization of normality', whereby social and infrastructural factors produce certain patterns of demand, which correspond to the normalisation of (unsustainable) habits, routines, and everyday practices of consumption, for example, around washing, showering and laundry, as well as travel and heating. Therefore, by tackling the systemic conditions and drivers of these practices, we can potentially reconfigure systems in a more sustainable way.

In this sense, sociological and social practice hold great promise in understanding the enabling conditions for achieving sustainable lifestyles by analysing the reverse: the systems, infrastructures, and cultures that produce and reproduce unsustainable consumption. As Giddens explains, consumption choices in today's complex world are not one-stop, quick-fire actions, but rather relate to deeper self-identity, and represent, 'decisions not only about how to act but who to *be*' (1991: 81, emphasis added). This need to express self-identity in consumerist cultures via predominantly materialistic means (earning more to spend more), represents one of the greatest challenges for achieving sustainable behaviour change, and explains why green consumerism has provided such a successful placeholder for those seeking to improve their eco-credentials without the need to step out of the prevailing acquisitive growth paradigm.

It also raises the question of how to create a counterculture to consumerism when its reach is so pervasive. This has brought a renewed focus on inequality, excess consumption, and green aesthetics (Urry, 2010; vans, 2019; Dietz el al., 2020; Soper, 2020). As Evans and Jackson explain: 'Consumerism is best understood as a cultural condition in which economic consumption becomes a way of life. It is a state of affairs in which more and more cultural functions are handed over to the activity of consumption such that it colonises more and more aspects of human experience' (2008: 6–7). Therefore, as long as consumerism, materialism, and economic growth continue to enjoy cultural supremacy, and until they are replaced by more sustainable and self-transcendent frameworks of meaning, such as well-being and sufficiency, it will be an uphill struggle to divert behaviours in a sustainable direction. To this end, Dietz et al. (2020) propose that sociology has a role to play in unpicking the contextual conditions driving variations in GHG emissions between and within countries (macro), corporations/social actors (meso), and individuals (micro), to gain a better understanding of what drives some actors to act differently under similar social, political, and economic institutional conditions.

Shove believes that the dominant A(ction), B(ehaviour), C(hoice) paradigm has been so successfully sustained in governance and policy discourses because it serves the needs and interests of policymakers to put responsibility for action (and inaction) primarily at the door of individuals, rather than questioning the institutions and systems that sustain it (2010: 1283). As applied to sustainable behaviour research, she warns against assuming that evidence of apparently successful interventions in one sphere (e.g. on smoking, littering, seat belt use) is necessarily transferable to other contexts, which may result in misguided policy and outcomes. She suggests greater academic and policy attention be paid to the evolution of 'envirogenic' environments that result in more self-reinforcing sustainable behaviours, and cites the success of the more holistic approaches taken in public health and urban planning spheres to tackle obesity, where diet and exercise are understood to be shaped by social, institutional and infrastructures, as well as reflected in broader 'patterns of time and mobility' (Shove, 2010).

In the energy sector, Shove & Walker (2010) argue for understanding the dynamics underlying demand where there has been a disproportionate focus on technological innovations and systems of supply in socio-technical transitions and energy governance (Royston et al., 2018). Similarly, with respect to energy use customs, Rinkinen et al. challenge mainstream energy policy and research by questioning their assumptions about energy demand underlying normative terms, such as 'energy efficiency' (implying a certain level of demand is necessary), without exploring what a sufficient level may be (2019: 125). Here social cleavages are instructive too, with affluent households found to be investing in energy efficiencies, and poorer homes reducing energy use through lifestyle adjustments. Sometimes devices, notionally aimed at improving efficiency, might also (counterproductively) allow people to increase energy consumption in other domains as part of the rebound effect.

Despite the undoubted capacity of social practice theory to, first, help identify barriers to scaling, second, capture the complexity of relationships between social and physical structures, and, third, offer a comprehensive framework for evaluating the shortcomings of behavioural interventions, the *practical applicability* of the approach for informing policy has been criticised as offering little more than general advice to 'tak[e] social norms a bit more seriously as influences of behaviour' (Jackson, 2005: 63). Further, its limitations in helping shape the precise design of target interventions have also been highlighted, given that so little is yet understood about the evolution and dynamics of social practices. Evans et al. (2012), however, firmly rebuff this critique by presenting a series of 'emergent programmes of practice-based interventions' in the housing, food and mobility sectors, suggesting that successful programmes need to be coordinated, attentive to webs of practice, and adaptive.

Taking an integrative theoretical approach may, therefore, be a potential way forward. Although coming from a predominantly psychological disciplinary perspective, Nash et al. argue that social practice theory has the potential to improve understandings of how to foster sustainable lifestyles, and highlight the value of paying greater attention to social norms in generating climate-conscious, spillover behaviours, specifically, 'via carriers of practice, materiality, and through relationships between practices within wider systems of practice' (2017: 1). Moreover, although psychological approaches focus on the features of the immediate environment in which behaviours are habitual, there are important linkages with sociological practice, which explores the broader elements of social and structural environments in which practices are normalised (Darnton et al., 2011; Southerton, 2013).

Political Economy

Though there is some common ground with sociological approaches, political economists argue that approaches to consumption from economics, sociology, and psychology tend to 'ignore structural elements of the problem grounded in political and economic systems' (Princen et al., 2002: ix), where economists equate consumption with the 'demand function' and sociologists view it as an expression of identity and search for meaning in modern society (Giddens, 1991). From this perspective, consumption is viewed, 'not just as an individual's choice among goods, but as a stream of choices and decisions winding its way through the various stages of extraction, manufacture and final use, embedded at every step in social relations of power and authority' (Princen et al., 2002: 12).

Traditionally, political economists often focus on production (and struggles over who controls it) as the root of social change and are often critiqued for their reductionism and neglect of questions of culture, despite advances in cultural political economy (Jessop, 2010). They tend to view consumption largely in relation to the role of debt and crises of under-consumption for growth in a capitalist society (Wilhite, 2016). In relation to socio-technical transitions, there is an emphasis on 'lock-in' (Unruh, 2000) and regime resistance (Geels, 2014), as well as cultures of consumption (Princen et al., 2002; Dauvergne, 2008) that fuel and sustain consumption through (among other things) Fordist production models that require mass consumption, or more recently, debt-fuelled spending, and the role of advertising in sustaining demands and aspirations that are unsustainable.

As political economists, they are alert to the challenges that attempts to check consumerism face. Maniates notes, for example, 'advertisers have the full weight of Western liberal tradition in their corner. To be anti-advertising is to be anti-democratic, if not anti-market' (2002: 207). Part of scaling behaviour then is also about how to scale back unsustainable behaviours. Capstick et al. (2015) suggest, for example, that a more radical approach to reducing personal emissions in line with the sorts of parameters described earlier would need to challenge dominant norms and givens in (capitalist) society. For example,

> to deliberately promote reduced consumption as a means of lowering people's embedded carbon emissions . . . immediately collides with powerful

and deep-rooted political and economic assumptions about the importance of consumer spending as a means of driving economic growth. Indeed, the paradigm of economic growth is itself used as a proxy for societal well-being (Capstick, 2015: 7).

This speaks to a much deeper political economy challenge around the very function of the state in a capitalist society: to reproduce the conditions for the expansion of capital, even if that means increasing social inequalities and environmental degradation. Fuelling growth through advertising and consumer spending is central to this way of organising the economy. From this point of view, therefore, individual behaviour change is insignificant when set against the need for 'de-growth' and structural change in the very purpose of economic activity away from growth as the *means* and *end* of state policy, as opposed to prosperity or well-being for instance (Jackson, 2011, 2021). Given the power of incumbent actors, this is not an easy undertaking (Fuchs et al., 2019). Nor does it sit easily with the need for rapid change. Indeed, political economists are often far better at accounting for why things *do not* change, rather than how and when they can (Newell & Simms, 2020).

In terms of *global* political economy, though many of these connections are often under-explored in existing scholarship, attention would focus on the global and historical patterns of exchange, extraction, and uneven development that underpin contemporary inequalities in consumption and their ecological consequences (Brand & Wissen, 2021). These relate to historical inequities and patterns of colonialism aimed at extracting resources and wealth for the benefit of the Global North, but which persist through unfair terms of trade, patterns of regulation and global governance, which lock-in privileged market access for mobile transnational companies (Newell, 2001). Hence, the 'cheap' oil, cotton, or meat that features highly in the lifestyles of the affluent is under-priced in social and environmental terms regarding the costs it passes on to society and ecosystems, both now and in the future. These goods can only be consumed on a large scale because of structural inequalities, which must be addressed as part of a broader project of transforming the economy away from its current destructive path.

Where such approaches are useful is in pointing to the need to disrupt power relations and get to the roots of unsustainable consumption by addressing economic policy, the conduct of elites, the power of advertising, rebalancing work and incomes, as well as challenging concentrations of wealth and the control over production and politics. Many scholars working on behaviour change within this tradition attend to the intrinsic links between sustainable production and consumption. They also tend to place more emphasis on the role of social movements as the disruptors of consumer culture and the sites of alternatives. This can be through protest against particular products or business practices, the co-production of 'civil regulation' of the private sector through codes of conduct, certification and the like (Newell, 2001), or building of alternatives as 'prosumers' get involved in community energy production and local food networks, for example (Seyfang, 2006).

The focus, however, is often the system rather than the individual. For example, applying a political economy analysis to a systems provision approach, Mattioli et al. (2020) show that research on car dependence often lacks analysis of the political-economic factors underpinning car-dependent societies – which include the power of the car industry, the provision of car infrastructure over affordable public transport, the political economy of urban sprawl, cultures of car consumption and car dependence being entrenched through the law (Böhm et al., 2006; Paterson, 2006). These, they argue, are crucial elements to the maintenance of car dependence, the reproduction of carbon lock-in (Unruh, 2000) and legislative lock-in (Taylor, 2021), which need to be challenged and reversed if sustainable lifestyles are to flourish.

A final contribution of political economy analysis is to provide an account of historical precedents of large-scale shifts in behaviour, including ones initiated and enforced by the state. For example, Newell and Simms (2020: 11) argue that '[w]hen they choose to do so, states can play a proactive role in dramatically and rapidly shifting cultural practices'. Dramatic levels of resource conservation during the Second World War were achieved by rationing around household waste reduction, the conversion of land from livestock to cereals and the establishment of 1.7 million allotments to encourage people to 'dig for victory'. They suggest, '[a]mazingly, from today's standpoint of rampant mass consumerism, efforts were invested by the state in de-legitimising wasteful consumption' (Newell & Simms, 2020: 12). Railway companies advertised that needless travel is a crime, while the UK Ministry of Fuel and Power appealed to people not to 'squander electricity' and to 'save fuel', 'mend, sew, repair'. In the USA, the Food Administration urged citizens not to 'waste food' and issued a list of instructions about how to do it which included: 'buy it with thought, cook it with care, use less wheat and meat, buy local foods, serve just enough, use what is left'.

In the United Kingdom, between 1938 and 1944, a complete revolution in consumption patterns was devised, implemented and the broad-based engagement of the population secured. Behaviours towards food, fuel, transport, and civic engagement altered rapidly. Andrew Simms suggests that apart from some well-known privations, an outcome of the rapid changes was not just a successful reduction of consumption and equalisation of access to resources among the population, it also saw a dramatic improvement in general health, life expectancy, and infant and maternal mortality (Simms, 2013). Political economy approaches would point then to the need to bring the state back into the debate about sustainable behaviours, as the only institution with a specific mandate and the means to advance and protect the public interest. This would be a broader project of re-commoning: to socialise control over the provisions of key services that have been ceded to the private sector under neoliberalism.

A related set of insights from political science and political economy focus on governance: a theme we emphasise throughout this Element. The governance of behaviour change, sustainable or otherwise, provides a potentially useful way of bridging individualist and systemic approaches. Interest in this area in part reflects thinking from other areas of environmental politics about the plurality of governance forms and mechanisms that characterise today's world and climate governance in particular (Bulkeley et al., 2014). For example, the idea of *'polycentric'* climate governance, associated with the late Elinor Ostrom (2010), suggests that the number of actors engaging in climate action has proliferated in recent years, partly in response to the slow progress of the global climate regime, but also because global climate initiatives, such as the Paris Agreement itself, have more recently called for the increased participation for non-state and sub-national actors (Hale, 2016). This has created new levels and entry points for engagement whereby,

> [e]ach unit within a polycentric system exercises considerable independence to make norms and rules within a specific domain (such as a family, a firm, a local government, a network of local governments, a state or province, a region, a national government, or an international regime)
>
> (Ostrom, 2010: 552).

This increases scope for informal, non-state actors to supplement, complement, as well as provide an alternative (radical) track to more formal, state-led governance processes, due to their: flexibility, capacity to self-organise locally, scope for building trusting relationships, potential for experimentation and innovation, and ability to incorporate feedbacks through experiential learning (Bulkeley et al., 2014). The role of polycentric governance in supporting sustainable behaviour change is also identified by Sovacool and Martiskainen (2020: 1) in their case studies exploring 'rapid and deep' transitions in household heating systems in China, Denmark, Finland, and the United Kingdom. They find, 'political and governance architecture can be just as salient as technical innovation and development in stimulating transitions', and identify six features of polycentric governance that help to facilitate change in their four cases: equity (sharing costs and benefits); inclusivity and local involvement; integrating information and feedbacks; enhancing ownership and accountability (of producers and users); involving multiple stakeholders with overlapping responsibilities across scales; and building experimentation and flexibility into the process.

Conceptually, multilevel and multi-cited governance offers a way of bridging the gap between the agency of individuals and the power of structures, because it highlights the role of *informal* institutions (e.g. networks, social groups, norms, and practices), and explores how they interact with, and co-constitute *formal* ones (such as laws, rules, and procedures). It also provides a promising way of examining how ecosystems of transformation can operate as webs of interconnections, linking actors with systems via formal and informal institutions, across multiple arenas and levels.

Gaventa's 'power cube', which integrates levels, spaces, and forms of power, is useful in this regard. The three-dimensional model, first, illustrates that the *level* of engagement can be household, local, national, or global, as per the first axis of the cube. Second, the *'space'* where engagement takes place can be closed, invited, or created spaces, which Gaventa argues provides alternative 'third' spaces, 'where social actors reject hegemonic space and create spaces for themselves' (Gaventa, 2006: 27). Finally, drawing on Lukes (1974), Gaventa identifies three *forms* of power: (1) 'visible' power, which is accessible to a plurality of interests, usually exercised in formal political arenas; (2) 'hidden' power, only available to privileged interests who control the agenda and mobilise bias (in the case of sustainable behaviour change, fossil fuel industries, polluter elites, etc.); and (3) 'invisible' power, which achieves willing acquiescence from people by 'dominating ideologies, values and forms of behaviour,' using processes of socialisation, culture, and ideology to define what is appropriate and acceptable (Gaventa, 2006: 29). Operating in all of these '3 x 3' dimensions is necessary to achieve transformation, as Gaventa explains,

> [t]ransformative, fundamental change happens, I suggest, in those rare moments when social movements or social actors are able to work effectively across each of the dimensions simultaneously, i.e. when they are able to link the demands for opening previously closed spaces with people's action in their own spaces; to span across local and global action, and to challenge visible, hidden and invisible power simultaneously. Just like the Rubik's cube, successful change is about getting each of the pieces on each dimension of the cube to align with each other, simultaneously (Gaventa, 2006: 30).

Clearly, many aspects of this model chime with the different theoretical perspectives we have introduced, which together can be viewed as parts of a whole ('cube'). At the risk of caricature, behaviourists focus on the individual and household levels and tend to focus on where actions and arenas are more visible; sociologists emphasise habitual and collective practices, and implicit social systems; and political economists hone in on the macro political and economic realms, and the hidden and invisible circuits of structural and institutional power that pervade the system. In this way, it is apparent that the four main disciplinary perspectives we have laid out in this section operate at different analytical levels, and present broadly distinct ways of approaching the question of behaviour change: how to understand it, scale it, and make it more sustainable. Though they each assume different units of analysis, theories of change and potential points of intervention, there are areas of complementarity and overlap that are useful – indeed necessary – for understanding and engaging with the complex mosaic of societal behaviour change. Furthermore, they underscore the importance of 'governance', which analytically straddles all of these levels, spaces, and forms of power, especially when the concept is broadened to include not only formal politics, institutions, and policy realms but also their informal and hybrid guises too.

In the end, however, academic theories on the subject of behaviour change, and how and when it might be possible to scale it, need to be closely integrated with observations and reflections based on lived experiences to fully appreciate the way that things happen in practice. In the remaining sections, we unpack what this means for scaling behaviour change.

4 Leverage and Tipping Points

The severity of the climate crisis, the urgency of action now required to address it, and the sheer scale of disruption that humanity is set to experience over the coming decades is accelerating interest in the idea of leverage and tipping points to facilitate transformative change.

In this section, we focus on political tipping points and moments of accelerated change as they apply to the challenge of scaling behaviour change. These can be identified as ruptures in the social contract, habit discontinuity events, the re-framing of social issues, and novel re-constellations of actors and institutions in advancing behaviour change. This is less a recipe or modelling of a change process (as with IAMs and some approaches to tipping points) and more an account of when and how political shifts can occur, drawing on work on the politics and political economy of socio-technical transitions and their histories, as well as emerging transdisciplinary work around leverage and tipping points for sustainability transformation (Leventon et al., 2021; Tàbara et al., 2021).

The question of scaling suggests the need not just to work across all sites of behaviour change, and all approaches to engaging types of behaviour change from the individual to systemic, but also to consider leverage and tipping points in these ecosystems of change where change can be deepened and accelerated to the greatest extent. For example, Leventon et al. delve into the complexity of system scales, and how interventions at one scale, such as at the individual level, can impact changes at other scales, such as food production (2021). They argue that the sheer contextual variety of leverage points – across disciplines, places, and timeframes – is 'testament to the contribution that a leverage points perspective can make in understanding how to create fundamental systems change towards sustainability' (Leventon et al., 2021). For these writers, therefore, an appreciation of leverage points can 'introduce conceptual clarity to untangle some of the deeper questions around which system we are engaging with, whose system counts, and whose sustainability we are seeking to create' (Leventon et al., 2021: 712).

Firstly, let's explore the concept of tipping points. The idea of there being tipping points in systems originally came from the natural sciences (Lenton & Williams, 2013), but has been adopted by social scientists to understand social tipping points (STPs) (Centola et al., 2018; Otto et al., 2020, 2020a; Smith et al., 2020), including in relation to decarbonisation (Smith et al., 2020). Social tipping points have been defined within an socio-ecological system (SES) as the point 'at which a small quantitative change inevitably triggers a non-linear change in the social component of the SES, driven by self-reinforcing positive-feedback mechanisms, that inevitably and often irreversibly lead to a qualitatively different state of the social system' (Otto et al., 2020: 3).

Otto et al. analyse the potential of social tipping interventions to 'activate contagious processes of rapidly spreading technologies, behaviours, social norms, and structural reorganization within their functional domains that we refer to as social tipping elements (STEs)' (2020: 2354). STEs then are 'sub-domains of the planetary socio-economic system where the required disruptive change may take place and lead to a sufficiently fast reduction in anthropogenic greenhouse gas emissions' (Otto et al., 2020: 2354). Interestingly, very few of the STEs identified directly relate to behaviour change. Only the call to strengthen climate education and engagement comes closest to behaviour change, and even there the assumed causality is very indirect, even though 'lifestyles' are listed as a social tipping point element and embrace of fossil-free consumption and vegetarian diets are mentioned as examples. The STEs they focus on include things such as removing fossil-fuel subsidies, constructing carbon-neutral cities, divestment from fossil fuels and disclosure of GHG emissions.

Applied to behaviour change, the idea of 'tipping points' alludes to the way in which behaviours become socially unacceptable or new behaviours become widespread and diffuse. At times these can be mandated, such as with mask wearing during the global pandemic, or pursued through regulation (such as wearing seat belts in cars, drink driving bans, or bans on smoking), though they are often predated by years of social campaigning and cultural stigmatisation through advertising and public information campaigns. On other occasions, behavioural trends accelerate, such as around the adoption of meat-free diets, where the market share for vegan products suddenly surges despite years of awareness about the environmental and animal welfare issues associated with the meat and livestock industry. Moments of crisis are thought to create opportunities to accelerate these shifts. It is no coincidence that many of the most popular and frequently referenced examples of mass behaviour change come from the Second World War, around rationing, local food production, and efforts to eliminate food waste, for example, where there is clear evidence of radical reductions in consumption (Simms, 2013).

A challenge in terms of drawing too many parallels from the experience of rationing that is often referred to in debates about sustainable living, is that while publics may have been willing to make temporary sacrifices for a war effort, societies may be less willing to do so as part of a new norm of reduced consumption as would be required to tackle climate change (Newell & Simms, 2020). Rationing only lasted during the war, then consumption rapidly increased afterwards. That said, during the 2007–2008 financial crisis people looked to radical measures to reduce public spending. This involved working less with the benefit of reducing stress. Utah in the USA introduced a four-day week for public sector workers and studied what happened. There was a 14 per cent drop in CO_2 by closing public buildings for the extra day, well-being rose and absenteeism dropped as workers were happier (Simms, 2013: 393). Although they changed the time period for accessing public services, a third of the public thought services had improved. In many ways, the search for relevant examples depends on the type of change we are interested in. Many of the examples mentioned here are of attempts by governments to persuade individuals to change behaviour. But if we think of collective action in pursuit of radical and disruptive political change, examples from the civil and women's rights movements, as well as those seeking to end apartheid or promote fossil fuel divestment, become more relevant, where it is the state and its links to incumbent business interests that need to be disrupted more than individual behaviours.

A second concept, popular among sustainability science and systems analysts, as well as sustainability practitioners, is the idea of 'leverage points' (Meadows, 1999; Birney, 2021; Leventon et al., 2021). These are places within a system where a small shift in one part of the system can generate changes across the system as a whole, where the greatest changes come about by targeting the deeper system properties, like the overarching paradigm, rather than shallower system properties. Supporting 'inner transformations' and shifts in values and world views often involve culturing change over longer time frames. It requires us to attend to 'mindsets, values, worldviews, beliefs, spirituality and human–nature connectedness' (Woiwode et al., 2021: 841). As Davelaar argues (2021: 727), 'transformation needs us to see and reconceive the human–world bond through the systemic lens of dynamic inclusion, aliveness, purpose and value'.

But it is the interaction of leverage points that is the key. Targeted interventions at one leverage point can have a knock-on effect upon other leverage points within the system, as shifts take place over time (Jiren et al., 2021). Existing literature points to the need for more transformational approaches and frameworks that draw upon different disciplines to identify the boundaries of the system, the stakeholders involved and how they are connected to one another, but questions remain about how these will be achieved in practice (Smith et al., 2020; Leventon et al., 2021). Echoing earlier reflections about the mismatch between carbon-intensive behaviour 'hotspots,' and where most policy interventions aimed at scaling behaviour change have been directed to date, Abson et al. (2016: 30) suggest,

> many sustainability interventions target highly tangible, but essentially weak, leverage points (i.e. using interventions that are easy, but have limited potential for transformational change). Thus, there is an urgent need to focus on less obvious but potentially far more powerful areas of intervention.

This approach to identifying 'deep leverage points' is inspired by the work of Donella Meadows (1999) on the hierarchy of intervention points for achieving change (see Figure 2). It suggests the need to go beyond incremental change aimed at adjusting policy parameters, and towards rules, structures, values, and paradigms, implying a role for interventions informed by the types of psychological, sociological, and political economy thinking reviewed earlier and the future intervention points we review in Section 5. Moreover, identifying leverage points requires us to embrace the complexity of systems, their different scales, and the ways in which they interact and integrate. By engaging with the complexity of systems and their scales, and taking a leverage points perspective, the binary between systems change and individual behaviour change can be conceptually challenged. Troeger and Reese, for instance, argue that individuals are both systems themselves and agents that can enact change within broader systems (2021). Others emphasise the embedded nature of systems, whereby narrower systems, like the provision of energy, are embedded in broader systems that shape and influence them, such as the techno-institutional system of fossil fuel extraction (Unruh, 2000; Schlaile et al., 2020). As such,

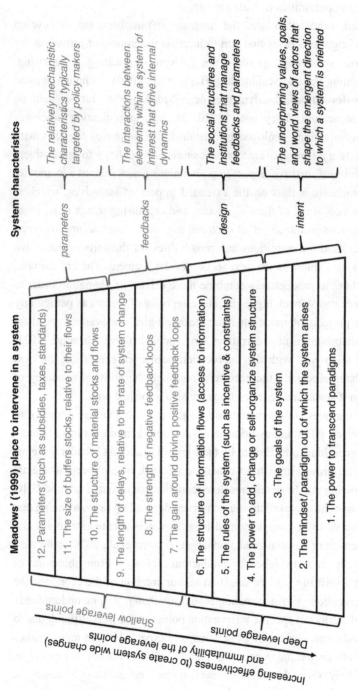

Figure 2 Intervention points in a system

Source: *Meadows (1999)*

System characteristics

The relatively mechanistic characteristics typically targeted by policy makers — parameters

The interactions between elements within a system of interest that drive internal dynamics — feedbacks

The social structures and institutions that manage feedbacks and parameters — design

The underpinning values, goals, and world views of actors that shape the emergent direction to which a system is oriented — intent

Meadows' (1999) place to intervene in a system

12. Parameters (such as subsidies, taxes, standards)
11. The size of buffers stocks, relative to their flows
10. The structure of material stocks and flows
9. The length of delays, relative to the rate of system change
8. The strength of negative feedback loops
7. The gain around driving positive feedback loops
6. The structure of information flows (access to information)
5. The rules of the system (such as incentive & constraints)
4. The power to add, change or self-organize system structure
3. The goals of the system
2. The mindset/paradigm out of which the system arises
1. The power to transcend paradigms

Shallow leverage points

Deep leverage points

Increasing effectiveness (to create system wide changes) and immutability of the leverage points transformations in one system can trigger transformations in connected systems, creating opportunities to scale change.

Other recent scholarship uses the language of amplification to develop a typology of eight processes that aim to increase the impact of initiatives for transformation: stabilising, speeding up, growing, replicating, transferring, spreading, scaling up, and scaling deep (Lam et al., 2020). Although applied to urban transformations, the dynamics described help shed further light on approaches to scaling. They note (2020: 3) that 'amplification processes describe diverse actions deployed by sustainability initiatives together with other actors (e.g., from government, business, or society) to purposively increase their transformative impact (e.g., initiating a new initiative in another city). The emphasis is thus on the extended impact of initiatives, which is created when new ways of thinking, doing, and organising things (e.g., practices, processes, or products) get adopted and amplified'. Such an approach can help us understand the conditions and possibilities for the sorts of purposive interventions we explore in the next section of the Element. The critical task, however, is how to productively combine these drivers of change in order to scale it. Linnér and Wibeck highlight four categories of drivers as particularly important to projects of transformation: 'technological innovations, political economy redistribution, new narratives, and transformative learning' (2021: 889). These align well with the intervention points we explore in the next section, perhaps especially the need to foreground the political economy of redistribution if sustainability transitions are also to be just ones.

However, many existing approaches to activate these leverage points or to generate positive, STPs and avoid negative ecological tipping points (or feedback effects) continue to be limited by their failure to address broader systems. Energy use and growth are almost exactly correlated, with a recent academic synthesis showing that large and absolute reductions of resource use and GHG emissions cannot be achieved through observed decoupling rates, meaning that decoupling needs to be complemented by sufficiency-oriented strategies and strict enforcement of absolute reduction targets (Haberl et al., 2020), otherwise efficiency gains are outweighed by production increases. From this point of view, absent a shift in the basic direction and orientation of the economy, the value of interventions aimed at scaling behaviour change will be undermined.

Isolating the effect of specific intervention points is also very difficult due to the nested and connected nature of systems, and especially as in many studies the point of reference is the impact of a 'bundle' of interventions. For example, Dietz et al. (2009) show that interventions that *combine* mass-media messages, household- and behaviour-specific information, and communication through individuals' social networks and communities could lead to reductions of

20 per cent in household direct emissions. Moreover, they suggest this can be achieved in less than 10 years, with little or no reduction in household well-being. In terms of engagement or awareness raising (or what is sometimes called 'social marketing') rather than deeper behaviour change, the effect is sometimes easier to capture.

Predicting when such tipping points might occur or isolating particular leverage points within complex systems, when there are so many intervening variables at play, is a fraught endeavour. Indeed, even in tipping points research, such moments are described qualitatively, not quantitatively: when a certain behaviour goes from being 'a minor tendency' to a 'major practice' (Otto et al., 2020), as perhaps with the rise of veganism in recent years in some parts of the world as part of a broader uptake of plant-based diets. Nevertheless, others do focus on key thresholds. Some suggest between 17 and 20 per cent market or population share can be enough to constitute a tipping point and become the dominant pattern (Otto et al., 2020). Extinction Rebellion activists often point to the work of Chenoweth and Stephan (2011) on the percentage of the population that need to engage in civil disobedience for it to have disruptive effects, while transition scholars suggest a transition in systems provision can be said to have occurred when 50 per cent market share is secured (Fouquet, 2016). Centola et al. (2018), meanwhile, explore experimental evidence of how minority groups can reach a critical mass sufficient to induce social change. They suggest that a committed group of 25 per cent can be sufficient to overturn social convention within the total population.

It clearly matters, however, *where, when*, and *who* leads such change. Some authors argue that it must be the 'right' share of the population, including well-connected influential people, trendsetters, and other types of social leaders with a high degree of agency (Otto et al., 2019: 3). This relates back to psychological understandings of the value of modelling, framing, and trust for promoting behavioural contagion. It also highlights the need to better integrate political actors as drivers of change, something well-versed in governance perspectives that point to the value of leadership, pioneers, and policy entrepreneurs (Liefferink & Wurzel, 2017; Petridou & Mintrom, 2020), as well as political economy understandings of power as being embedded by key actors in critical structures (highlighted in Section 3). This also speaks to the importance of intermediaries, brokers, and facilitators in leading by example and of improving the efficacy of targeted strategies. From the field of social innovation, for example, Westley underlines the potential for institutional entrepreneurs as, 'important brokers for connecting people and networks ... providing leadership, building trust, developing visions, and sensemaking', as well as eroding the resilience of dominant institutional systems by presenting, 'viable shadow alternatives and niche regimes' (Westley et al., 2011: 762, 771).

On timing, as Otto et al. (2020: 7) acknowledge, '[s]ince social-ecological dynamics are subject to complex processes that cannot be fully anticipated, it is not possible to predict when and where exactly tipping points will be crossed'. The key issue is the 'prefigurative' politics: preparing the ground for when political opportunities arise to scale ambitions. As E. F. Schumacher puts it (1973: 31): 'Perhaps we cannot raise the winds. But each of us can put up the sail, so that when the wind comes we can catch it.' Some of the advocacy around anti-fossil fuel norms (Green, 2018) can be thought of in this way, eroding the social licence to operate of the fossil fuel industry and socialising the idea of production limits. At the same time, changes to goals and rules are proposed as deeper leverage points around demands for a multilateral framework on supply-side policies to leave large swathes of remaining fossil fuels in the ground (Newell & Simms, 2019). When more rapid and disruptive change of a positive nature occurs, for it to become embedded, socialised, and normalised, it needs to be institutionalised or supported by governance innovations that seek to ensure the durability and longevity of change. Even the prospect of regulation can be a key driver of change. But besides rights-based struggles, campaigns to tackle air pollution, ozone depletion, and biodiversity loss, all demonstrate national and international legal protection often comes on the back of years or decades of advocacy.

From transition studies we can see how niche behaviours get mainstreamed. A large body of work on socio-technical transitions accounts for transitions in the provision of services such as mobility, heating, and cooling. It describes how shifts occur whereby 'niches' disrupt dominant 'regimes', often enabled by changes in the broader 'landscape' that can accelerate these shifts (Geels, 2005) (see Figure 3). It combines analysis of social and technological elements so that things as diverse as practices, behaviours, governance institutions, innovation and finance, and shifts in population can be included in the analysis. Examples include larger shifts from coal to oil, as well as shifts in cooking practices and transport behaviours. Different bodies of work place different emphasis on the key factors driving change, but there has been a move to include more analysis of governance and justice dimensions and to place questions of power and politics more centrally in explanations of the speed, direction, and depth of transitions (Sovacool, 2021).

What is interesting and relevant to our enquiry is that questions of scale and pace are gaining more attention in transition studies (Sovacool, 2016; Newell & Simms, 2020). It might also be possible to understand key tipping points in behaviour in relation to the dynamic that exists between niches, dominant

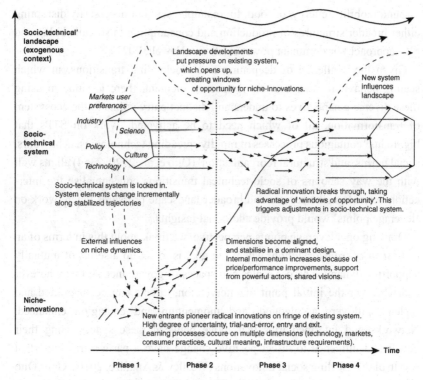

Figure 3 The multilevel perspective
Source: Reproduced from Geels et al. (2017)

regimes and practices, and the ways in which landscape pressures (around climate change) can disrupt regimes and move niche behaviours (around plant-based diets or cycling) to become more mainstream (see Figure 3).

It is important to acknowledge though that each of these perspectives proposes, and is underpinned by, a different theory of change that would suggest different entry points in the ecosystem of transformation. For scholars interested in tipping points, the issue is how to anticipate the creation of moments of disruption and amplify them whereafter widespread social change becomes possible. Those writing about leverage points, meanwhile, highlight the need for paradigm shifts and changes to the rules and power relations as points of 'deep leverage' – hence cultural and power shifts come to the fore. Some such scholars would also highlight how interventions at one scale, such as at the individual level, can impact changes at other scales (Leventon et al., 2021). Transition scholars usefully explore the prospects of accelerating transitions (Cameron et al., 2018), but find themselves subject to critiques that they neglect questions of power by focussing more on questions of innovation and technological breakthrough as crucial to changing systems of service provision (around mobility, energy, or food, for example) without necessarily disrupting either broader structures of production and consumption (a so-called plug and play approach) or dominant power relations (Newell, 2021).

Given the challenge of deepening and accelerating transitions, in which scaling behaviour change is one important element, there is value in using these diverse perspectives to understand distinct entry points in the ecosystem of transformation, all of which need to be activated. Work on STPs that highlights 'contagious processes of rapidly spreading technologies, behaviours, social norms, and structural reorganization' (Otto et al., 2020: 2354) aligns well with the way scholars of socio-technical transitions conceptualise the interaction between niche-regime and broader landscape pressures where work on 'leverage points' would provide additional insights.

Drawing on a leverage points perspective, we think about this in terms of an *ecosystem of transformation*, where the goal is to set up a series of mutually supportive dynamics across scales and spaces of governance so that wherever and whatever the initial point of intervention, effects can be magnified and scaled, spillovers accelerated, and momentum and contagion enhanced. Networks and intermediaries that move between these spaces using their power and influence to effect positive change have a particularly important role to play in scaling social innovations (Westley & Antadze, 2010). Or as Otto et al. (2020: 8) put it: 'The social tipping dynamics are likely to spread through adaptive networks of interactions rather than via straightforward cause–effect systems.' This relates to our above-mentioned point about 'mutual accountability' and 'reciprocity' and the ratcheting up of ambitions and commitment over time as states, communities, cities and businesses push one another to do more.

There are various points of intervention in the system of consumption (or what we refer to later as the 'chain of consumption') (see Table 2) which, taken together, could help to bring about the scale of behaviour change prescribed. They are informed in different ways by the four approaches to behaviour change reviewed earlier. These run from the generation of demand, to shifts in corporate practice and government decision-making, to citizen action, with a view to setting in train virtuous circles where reduced and shifting patterns of demand within limits set by governments are met in innovative ways by business and civil society, increasingly organised around goals of 'plentitude' and well-being rather than growth and increases in economic throughput.

5 Future Intervention Points

As things stand under a business-as-usual scenario, we are headed for 2.7 degrees of warming by the end of the century, with catastrophic consequences

Table 2 The chain of consumption

Approach	Instrument	Example
Supply-side policies	Bans, moratoria, phase outs of new production	Oil moratoria in Costa Rica, New Zealand, Denmark, France, Belize
		Bans on fracking
		Phase outs of petrol and diesel cars
		Bans on ozone-depleting and climate warming chemicals (CFCs, etc.)
Agreeing limits	Rationing Individual allowances and carbon budgets	WWII examples of rationing
		Proposals for individual carbon budgets
	Tradable emissions quotas[1]	Global contraction and convergence and Greenhouse Development Rights framework
Working less	Reducing length of the working week	Spain's trial of a four-day working week[2]
	Job sharing	UBI
	Paid care work	Utah state (USA)
		Germany's Kurzarbeit part-time working policy
		Grande-Synthe 'guaranteed social minimum' in France

[1] For more on David Fleming's proposal see www.flemingpolicycentre.org.uk/faqs/
[2] www.4dayweek.co.uk/

Table 2 (cont.)

Approach	Instrument	Example
Providing alternatives	Planning	Affordable public transport
	Infrastructures	Bike lanes and schemes for employees/support for EV Grants for EV installation and home insulation
	Subsidies and support	
Tackling the drivers of consumerism[3]	Restrictions on advertising in certain spaces (schools, hospitals) and at certain times	Grenoble, Chennai, São Paulo Restrictions on TV adverts before certain times to protect children.[4]
	Restrictions on targeting	Bans on tobacco advertising
	Restrictions on products	'Badvertising' campaigns on fossil fuel products such as SUVs
	Tax on advertising	1 per cent tax on all advertising[5]
Regulation and choice editing	Energy efficiency standards	Energy labelling for products/buildings
	Fuel efficiency standards for vehicles	Corporate Average Fuel Economy standards (USA)
	Rejecting carbon-intensive infrastructures	Restrictions on airport and road expansion, industrial farming
Self-regulation	Codes of conduct	Roundtables on responsible beef, soy, biofuels, etc.
	Supplier agreements	Targets by major retailers to decarbonise supply chains (Walmart, Tesco)
	Voluntary targets	Science-based targets[6]

---

[3] By some estimates 2018 global advertising spend is expected to top $630bn www.statista.com/topics/3201/ad-blocking/

[4] In Sweden, for example, TV advertising targeted at under-12s is banned on the grounds that children in that age range are unable to distinguish between programmes and advertising. See also Kasser and Linn (2016).

[5] Proposed by the Rapid Transition Taskforce.   [6] https://sciencebasedtargets.org/

Category	Subcategory	Example
Consumer information	Labelling	Soil Association standards for organic food
	Certification	Marine and Forestry Stewardship Council
	Carbon footprinting apps	BrewDog carbon footprint menu
		Carbon reduction apps like VYVE[7]
Education	School programmes	School sustainability leaders Eco-Schools (operating in 64 countries)
	City wide initiatives	Carbon Trust and Energy
	National programmes	Savings Trust (Switch off campaigns)
	Experiential learning	Forest schools
	Faith-based initiatives	Eco-synagogues, churches, and mosques
Voluntarism	Pledges	Meat-free Mondays
		Flight Free Year pledges
	Voluntary simplicity	Veganuary
		Ride share schemes
	Community organising	Repair cafes
Social mobilisation	Campaigns aimed at specific products/companies	OilWatch
	Generic campaigns	Boycott Exxon
	Campaigns for alternatives	Divestment movement

[7] www.bp.com/en_gb/united-kingdom/home/news/press-releases/vyve-a-new-way-to-understand-track-and-reduce-carbon-from-your-phone.htm]

Table 2 (cont.)

Approach	Instrument	Example
	Campaign in cultural spheres to challenge the social licence to operate	Shareholder action Fridays for Future/Youth Strike 4 Climate Fossil Fuel Non-Proliferation Treaty Support for wind energy (Possible) Art not Oil movement, Liberate Tate, Liberons le Louvre, Fossil Free Culture in the Netherlands
New goals and metrics	Going beyond conventional indicators of growth: Well-being/Prosperity/Plenitude as the goal	Happy planet index Gross National Happiness Well-Being index De-growth

for humanity and the ecosystems upon which we depend (UNEP, 2021). What has led to this scenario, and sustains it today, is unsustainable behaviours by governments, businesses, cities, and citizens. We clearly need dramatic and far-reaching change by *all* of these actors – though responsibility is, in the words of the UNFCCC, 'common but differentiated'.

One of the valuable things about approaches that emphasise power and politics is a recognition that things are not fixed and static, but rather transient, dynamic, and always subject to change – even for powerful incumbents. Hence, as well as showing how change is resisted and accommodated, political analysis of behaviour change also points to the possibilities of political reconfiguration and moments of disruption, especially when attentive to ecosystems of change and the possibility that multiple intervention points can be targeted simultaneously. Generating 'evidence-based hope' about the sorts of change that are possible (as well as desirable), grounded in examples from around the world today – as well as historical precedents – of when people organise to produce and consume food, energy, and water differently, or when systems of housing, transport, and finance get overhauled – can inspire new waves of action to address unsustainable consumption.[5]

This means identifying future interventions based on a clear understanding of distributed and uneven agency – where fissures and opportunities exist to advance change more rapidly and at scale. Analysis of this nature also suggests that theories and practices of change often overlap, interrelate, and amplify one another, causing ripple effects across the system and generating positive lock-ins through policy, legislation, and infrastructural and choice architectures. These ripple effects and changes are not singular, linear, or fixed, but often emergent, unfurling and co-evolving, with uncertain outcomes. Effective strategies for change recognise and act upon this, tailoring their strategies to specific political landscapes and contexts, fostering novel allies and coalitions around specific intervention points, while always being intuitive about the emergent nature of change.

Effective strategies for change must be cognisant of the shifting terrain on which interventions take place. As the past couple of years have shown, exogenous shocks have a tendency to shed light on entrenched social injustices and our (unevenly) shared vulnerability in the face of them. When the social contract is under pressure, and brought into question, windows of opportunity appear for potentially rapid and radical changes. This should also act as a reminder that many of these future interventions will be made on terrains and within governance landscapes that are not of our own choosing, nor where

---

[5] See the work of the Rapid Transition Alliance in this regard: www.rapidtransition.org/

we necessarily have the power to determine their conditions. Messy compromise, coalition-building, learning by doing is both inevitable and important.

It is often claimed that larger transitions will not be possible until citizens have demonstrated 'demand' for it, as politicians fear adopting unpopular measures and not bringing voters with them (Willis, 2018). Though frequently invoked to justify inaction, or delay further action, such claims need to be treated with extreme caution since most people are rarely asked about the level and pace of change they would like to see, or which of the costs associated with doing nothing they would be willing to bear. Moreover, as Moberg et al. (2019: 508) argue:

> the door for stronger government intervention is already 'half-open'. Governments already intervene with command-and-control measures in several high mitigation potential areas, so one may assume that this means there is already public acceptance for such intervention . . . . Respondents specifically call for stronger government intervention in the high mitigation potential areas as of yet receiving minor policy focus.

Yet government action needs to be complemented with behavioural change by individuals and communities if dangerous climate change is to be avoided, demonstrating a willingness to change and making it easier for politicians to show bold leadership. This has to be the basis of the social contract for addressing the climate emergency: each of us doing what we can, with the resources and means available to us, in the time we have available and in the spaces we are active in; supported, enabled, and enhanced by government action. We have witnessed decades of strategies and interventions aimed at bringing citizens on board with climate action. Some have achieved limited success. None, however, has been able to achieve the degree and scale of change now required. We are, therefore, in unchartered territory. New approaches are needed to get to the roots of unsustainable consumption and production in the current economy. Analytically, this means drawing on insights from the bodies of scholarship we reviewed in Section 3 to better understand multiple entry points for scaling behaviour change.

We propose some practical, complementary, and overlapping areas for action that flow from this. We organise these around the structural, systemic, and enabling approaches highlighted by Scoones et al. (2020) as being necessary for sustainable transformations, and which correspond to the political economy, sociological, and behavioural perspectives introduced in Section 3. As we have shown already, each highlights different units of analysis, arenas, and interventions for action. Building on our emphasis on ecosystems of transformation, we propose the simultaneous need for: (i) fundamental *structural* change, which addresses the economic, institutional, and ideological drivers of *un*sustanability, informed by political economy perspectives (rebalancing power and addressing historical legacies and injustices via alternative economic models); (ii) intentional *system* change, driven by insights from sociology, science and technology studies, and political science (just transitions, rethinking work, enabling infrastructures and governance for sustainability); and (iii) a more behavioural, agency-centred approach, targeted at *enabling actors* (social movements and bringing in new allies). The structural, systemic and enabling approaches for sustainable transformation are cross-cutting, complementary and reinforcing parts of an ecosystem of transformation, highlighting the necessity of simultaneous and plural interventions to scale sustainable behaviour change. This chimes with O'Brien and Sygna's (2013: 5) calls for greater recognition of the *interactions* within and between nested 'spheres of transformation', and acknowledges that transformations at one level (e.g. personal, political, or worldview) can not only trigger changes in other spheres, but crucially, 'some interventions are more powerful and effective than others'.

Structural Change

Rebalancing Power

If social transformation, of which behaviour change is merely one element (albeit an important one), is to be progressive, sustained, and sustainable, we need shifts in power within institutions and organisations from the community to the city, regional, national, and international level, as well as across the public and private sectors. Political tipping points, when they occur, need to ripple out across society, triggered by distinct intervention points that form part of an ecosystem of transformation. Connecting these intervention points through cycles of reciprocity is vital, whereby efforts by individuals, communities, and cities are matched by governmental and institutional leadership that creates space for bottom-up experimentation and integrates demands from social movements.

The key is to support an upward trajectory of ambition as cycles of reciprocal action by diverse actors drives deeper change. Ambitious government targets that incentivise the private sector to bring different technologies to market, which embolden city planners to design zero carbon cities and to build alternative infrastructures that make it easier for individuals to lead more sustainable lives could be transformative. Support to car-free cities and free or heavily subsidised public transport, supported by levies on polluting forms of transport, or government support for housing retrofit schemes to tackle energy poverty and reduce emissions, show what is possible. Likewise, mobilisations and demands from below by communities, youth movements, NGOs, and citizens participating in democratic spaces such as climate assemblies can push cities, businesses, and governments towards more ambitious climate action, as the multiple declarations of climate emergencies testify. As we have seen, individual, household, voluntary, and community action all make a difference in their own right, as well as creating space for bolder government action and new innovations from public and private actors by preparing the ground for more ambitious interventions. This is what we refer to as the virtuous cycles of reciprocity, where action by one set of actors enables action by another, ratcheting up ambition in a positive, upward 'spiral of sustainability' (Newell et al., 2021a).

This means, for example, that interventions to shift finance can bring about institutional changes and shifts in power relations which can enable behaviour change as new values take hold and alternative social and technological infrastructures are put in place to enable sustainable lifestyles. For example, advocacy around fossil fuel divestment, and pressure to withdraw state support through tax breaks, subsidies, and export finance helps to sever the ties between governments and incumbent industries, but it needs to be complemented by measures to address funding of political parties, directorships, and revolving doors between business and government. Once this happens, support can be built for more sustainable innovations and enable greater citizen control over energy systems, democratising oversight of key infrastructures and potentially inculcating more collective values. Likewise, behaviour change from below, combined with social mobilisation, can build momentum for lasting change. Movements around local food networks combined with advocacy against unsustainable forms of industrial agriculture, for example, can start to chart the way for an alternative pathway towards more sustainable agriculture. Institutions and political programmes, however, need to protect, generalise, and enforce those gains in order to become permanent.

Shifts towards alternative economies and lifestyles will not be possible – or will amount to little – without unsettling incumbents. As Fuchs et al. put it:

> informal and implicit theories of social change of scholars and activists in sustainable consumption and sustainable development fail to address power in a sufficiently explicit, comprehensive and differentiated manner and how that failure translates into insufficient understandings of the drivers of consumption and the potential for and barriers to absolute reductions. [...] Shying away from power allows the trends to play out to their logical and tragic ends. Asking about power, uncovering the hidden and exposing the inequitable is a civic obligation, a sustainability imperative, and a justice prerequisite (2016: 298, 306).

In practical terms this implies greater transparency, active roll-back, and advocacy around funding of political parties, secondments to government departments, revolving doors and commercial directorships through registries and rules on conflicts of interest, party funding, and the like (Newell & Martin, 2020). This needs to include corporate governance. Carbon Tracker (2020), for example, draw attention to fossil fuel executives' remuneration packages that, despite various net-zero pledges, still incentivise and reward unsustainable behaviours, such as increasing fossil fuel production or the size of reserves, which locks businesses into loops of continued expansion and exploration.

Fundamentally, therefore, the need to rebalance power needs to be brought to the forefront of the behaviour change debate. Strategies that challenge and undo incumbency are key, thereby exposing the close ties between rule-makers, major corporations, and those vested in shaping and expanding business-as-usual policies, while opening up alternative pathways to sustainability.

Alternative Economic Models

'Deep' scaling also requires a more sophisticated understanding of the social and cultural drivers of overconsumption: addressing advertising and the media's role in the normalisation and reification of high consumption behaviours. Regulation and 'choice editing' have a role to play whereby governments, businesses, and those with direct control over production restrict the availability of high carbon products and services such as private jets and sports utility vehicles, or using planning and building regulation to ensure better insulated homes. Such a shift would need to more fundamentally question cultural and social values around what it is to live a 'good life' informed by ideas of 'plentitude' (Schor, 2011), prosperity and well-being (Jackson, 2021), premised on the sharing of spaces, goods, and facilities rather than the individualisation of everything. This suggests the need for new indicators of progress, and new modes of organising economic relations, which focus on factors relating to sustainability and well-being, rather than economic output or labour productivity. On a more mundane but important level, it also suggests the need for IAMs to incorporate alternative economic models in order to create new mitigation pathways that do not rely on dubious and unrealistic assumptions around continued economic growth and technological development (Kuhnhenn, 2018; Keyßer & Lenzen, 2021).

As well as disrupting dominant representations of what is normal and possible with a view to how the economy is organised, it is also critical to articulate and showcase alternative ways of organising economic, political, and social life. It is difficult to comprehend the implications of the far-reaching and often abstract changes required to put human society on a sustainable pathway. But providing compelling and meaningful visions of the future is the first step to bringing them into being: moving from 'what is' to 'what if?' (Hopkins, 2019). By amplifying change and stories of change, we can expand the realms of possibility and broaden our collective horizons about what is 'normal', what is 'possible' and what is 'desirable'. There is an important role here for the arts and cultural industries to help people visualise and experience alternative futures, helping publics appreciate the tensions, trade-offs, and opportunities that will attend any attempt to move towards them, captured in the title of the arts installation 'We know not yet what we may be'.[6]

System Change

Just Transitions

To be effective and politically accepted, shifts in behaviour towards 1.5-degree lifestyles need to address social and economic justice and, at the very least, not further entrench existing inequalities or exacerbate the climate impacts already experienced by vulnerable populations (Patterson et al., 2018). In the words of the UN Secretary-General Guterres, 'a just transition is absolutely critical. We must recognize the human costs of the energy shift. Social protection, temporary basic income, re-skilling and upskilling can support workers and ease the changes caused by decarbonization' (Besheer, 2020).

Infrastructures, income, location, and social status all have a huge bearing on peoples' abilities to modify their behaviour. Almost 10 per cent of the global population continue to live in extreme poverty (World Bank, 2020), and lack basic food, housing, energy, and transport; in this context, 'lifestyle leapfrogging' can support the adoption of more sustainable pathways, avoiding fossil-fuel lock-in in the first place (Schroeder & Anantharaman, 2017). And across the board, key intervention points lie in creating enabling environments to facilitate sustainable practices among broad sections of society. Given that faith in the future – and individual perceptions of their capacity to act and influence that future – depend to a degree on livelihood security (Solovjew-Wartiovaara, 2021), addressing social, employment, and welfare provision will be critical alongside more traditional techno-environmental measures.

Efforts to promote behaviour change through just transitions also need to help remedy historical injustices, reinforcing the need for structural change highlighted earlier. There are important racial, class, and gender dimensions to access and responsibility, which all interventions need to explicitly address as

---

[6] https://metisarts.co.uk/projects/we-know-not-what-we-may-be/

part of efforts to decolonise the sustainable living debate. This will be a prerequisite to broadening the conversation about behaviour change beyond silos of privilege and spheres of voluntarism among those already conscious of, and committed to, environmental action and with the time and resources available to advance it. Promisingly, some governments are actively seeking to anticipate and address questions of social inclusion in relation to their net-zero strategies in which behaviour change has an important role to play.

Rethinking Work

Systems of work and questions of labour form a central, yet often neglected, part of the behaviour change debate. Changes to modes of working offer a powerful way of reducing pressure and stress in peoples' lives, as well as shifting patterns of consumption. As Simms argues (2010), 'moving towards a much shorter working week would help break the habit of living to work, working to earn, and earning to consume'. Due to the need to radically curtail consumption in industrialised nations in particular, work time reduction has the potential for scaling sustainable behaviour change across regions and sectors. Research suggests that work time reduction could shift behaviours in more sustainable directions by decreasing the scale of economic output and the environmental intensity of consumption patterns (Rosnick & Weisbrot, 2007; Knight et al., 2013) (including CO_2 emissions (Fitzgerald et al., 2018)), as well as improving life satisfaction and societal well-being (Borowy & Aillon, 2017) and nurturing more intrinsic values (Kasser, 2002). There is also a clear public health incentive for rethinking work, with long working hours contributing to over 745,000 deaths globally in 2016, a 29 per cent increase since 2000 (Pega et al., 2021). Despite the myriad of benefits, work time reduction has stalled in countries over recent decades and has begun to reverse, with only some exceptions (Schor, 2011; Burger, 2015). In 2016, approximately 488 million people around the world were exposed to long working hours, with significant social and health impacts (Pega et al., 2021).

The economic fallout and subsequent recovery from COVID-19 presents an opportunity to challenge traditional notions of work and introduce work time reduction measures, temporarily at first, but with a view to creating a permanent programme – especially considering trends such as looming automation in multiple sectors, stagnating economic growth, and the falling global demand for labour (Benanav, 2020). Germany's Kurzarbeit part-time working policy is an example, set to run through 2021, which allows business to pursue work time reduction during a time of structurally low aggregate demand (Contessi & Li, 2013). The Spanish government too has announced plans to pilot a four-day working week as a direct response to the economic challenges wrought by COVID-19 (Stone, 2021). In the United Kingdom, a study of 50,000 businesses concluded that a carefully designed four-day week could be introduced immediately and be financially viable for most firms with more than 50 workers (Elliott, 2020) and be backed by national legislation to protect the rights of workers.

Within the workplace there are opportunities to transform systems in favour of alternatives that can lay the foundations for scaling sustainable lifestyles. One emerging area of scholarship is around the need to bring more inclusive forms of ownership to the fore and, in the process, transform companies from vehicles of monopolising wealth extraction to economically coordinated, co-owned, and regenerative entities (Lawrence et al., 2020). Many of the prospective policies to re-common private business, such as maximum pay ratios and a ban on share buybacks, would transform our relationship to work, help address the inequalities between the polluter elite and the rest, and ultimately repurpose the company towards more social ends. There is also a role for leadership within organisations to 'walk-the-talk' on sustainable lifestyles (Avolio et al., 2009; Kraft-Todd et al., 2018).

However, enjoying a liveable income is also a foundational condition for creating a conducive backdrop to sustainable living. In recent years, workers across many sectors have seen structural changes that have led to the rise in the so-called gig-economy (e.g. zero-hour contracts and agency work), which, alongside cuts in welfare provision, have conspired to limit their control over their working hours and conditions (TUC, 2020). These factors are likely to make it difficult – and possibly economically unfeasible – for some to reduce their work hours or reorient their (unpaid) leisure time unless their economic security improves. Furthermore, in the domestic sphere, three-quarters of unpaid care work and two-thirds of care workers are women (and girls) (ILO, 2018). This represents another glaring barrier to participation in economic, social, and environmental activities, and highlights the need to bring informal systems into the formal economy to redress gender and other power imbalances, as the International Labour Office (ILO, 2018: xxix) explains, 'unpaid care work remains mostly invisible, unrecognized and unaccounted for in decision-making'. Interventions that seek to re-think the world of work must consider these heterogeneous experiences of care work and employment.

Governance for Sustainability

Overseeing transformative sustainable change calls for innovations in governance, to enhance coordination, broaden representation, and foster meaningful engagement in discussions about the complex trade-offs in getting to a zero-carbon economy. Cursory participation in behavioural change actions alone, referred to as 'shallow' scaling (Newell et al., 2021a), will not be sufficient to stimulate change at the speed or order necessary to stay within safe climatic limits. Rather, 'deep' scaling implies a more reciprocal, reflexive, and dynamic process between citizens, private actors, and governing institutions (Hall, 1993: 288). This may involve 'remaking' new democratic frameworks to govern climate change and using the multiple sites of decision-making afforded by 'polycentric' climate governance (Ostrom, 2010), where non-state actors and sub-national actors are increasingly, and more effectively, involved. This can help to integrate 'diverse knowledges', promote 'plural pathways', and 'take politics seriously' (Scoones et al., 2020). Evidence suggests that a more decentralised approach can also broaden scope for 'rapid and deep' household transitions to sustainability, promoting inclusion, accountability, and even equity (Sovacool & Martiskainen, 2020). The flexibility that polycentricity affords also makes it possible to incorporate innovations and feedbacks through experiential learning (Bulkeley et al., 2014; Jordan et al., 2018), which is integral to securing sustainable transformation as well as generating the reflexivity and experimentation that dynamic or 'spiral' scaling demands. Deliberative approaches can also help to enhance the legitimacy and social ownership of strategies to address climate change and support behaviour change (Dryzek & Niemeyer, 2019).

As noted earlier, a prerequisite for democratic (rather than imposed) societal transformation is deepening democracy itself through the revitalisation of systems of representation and participation, since existing structures privilege incumbent interests. Who decides which limits are set, by whom and how they are enforced, will determine the legitimacy and social acceptability of transitions. As Clarke et al. (2018: 4) state,

> [t]he 1.5 C target also requires lifestyle changes on a range of totemic issues like diet, personal travel and home heating in a relatively short period of time. Without public buy-in, these could prompt significant resistance. Given the short timescale, the infrastructure of public engagement needs to be put in place just as the infrastructure of policy change does.

Just as we need greater attention to be paid to input and throughput consumption, so too we need to bolster input and throughput legitimacy, that is, the *quality* of sustainability governance processes (Schmidt, 2013). From Citizen Assemblies and participatory budgeting, to the representation for future generations, there are many spaces for engagement and participation that can be activated or built. This would involve developing and refining more participatory tools for the deliberative development of scenarios for change, such as foresight exercises (Mao et al., 2020) driven by citizen's own values, concerns, and priorities. Such governance innovations can empower citizens and communities to make the changes required to live and thrive sustainably, challenging the dominant idea that individuals are passive consumers and instead recognise people and communities as *active citizens* with the agency to shape their own lives and the communities in which they live as part of broader ecosystems of transformation.

Research indicates that when spaces and processes are created for citizens to directly engage with, deliberate and shape public policy, the result is recommendations that recognise and seek to address the structural determinants of overconsumption and under-consumption (Kythreotis et al., 2019; Citizen's Assembly UK, 2020; Convention Citoyenne pour le Climat, 2020; Devaney et al., 2020; Muradova et al., 2020). The recent findings from Citizen Assembly UK, for instance, indicate that when individuals are informed and empowered to analyse, discuss, and debate collective responses to climate change, there is real appetite for radical change at the micro, miso, and macro level. Recommendations from the report include higher prices for frequent and further fliers, efforts to incentivise reduced meat consumption and scaling up active travel infrastructure (Citizen's Assembly UK, 2020). The concepts of fairness, accessibility, and affordability are prominent throughout all the Assembly's recommendations. Moreover, Ireland's citizen assembly resulted in similar recommendations, with the assembly calling for higher taxes on carbon-intensive activities (Muradova et al., 2020). Indeed, it is abundantly clear that there is appetite for radical changes (RESET, 2020), but such changes must be supported by a proactive and protective state.

Enabling Actors

Social Movements

We have argued that the behaviours of states, business, cities, and individuals need to change. But social movements have a vital role to play in advancing progressive change. The past few years have seen a proliferation of social movements crystalising around environmental and climate issues globally that have emphasised the potential of both collective action and behavioural contagion. Individual behaviour change can be the first step to more active engagement with processes of change, including social mobilisation (Willis & Schor, 2012; Kalmus, 2017; Leiserowitz, 2019; De Moor & Verhaegen, 2020; Kalmus, 2017; Leiserowitz, 2019). Movements like Extinction Rebellion and Fridays for Future have been instrumental in shaping the public discourse around climate action, but are not the only social movements enacting change in their communities, with a variety of community and transition groups active within the field of sustainable behaviour change.

What all these movements have in common is that they are dynamic and leverage a networked approach to change, utilising non-violent protest and new-media platforms to expand their reach and connecting action across scales of governance. While the goals and modes of operation of some social movements may not entice action from the majority of the population, they are vital in setting the agenda on certain matters of policy and the public framing of specific issues. For example, it is hard to imagine governments around the world declaring climate emergencies and legislating for net-zero if it hadn't been for Greta Thunberg, the Fridays for Future youth-strikes, and protests by Extinction Rebellion.

Social mobilisation is also a key ingredient in enabling and accelerating behaviour change by harnessing the consumer power of citizens. As Michael Maniates puts it, 'individual consumption choices are environmentally important, but their control over these choices is constrained, shaped and framed by institutions and political forces that can be remade only through collective action' (2002: 65). Sustainable Community Movement Organisations (SCMOs) provide an important focus on political consumerism by mobilising citizens primarily via their purchasing power (Forno & Graziano, 2014: 142). Political consumerism aims at re-socialising 'wrongdoers' and changing business activities through the 'power of numbers'. An increasing number of movement organisations acting regionally, nationally, and globally have started to incorporate this into their repertoire of action.

This type of activism builds on longer histories of 'civil regulation': civil society-based regulation of private actors through liberal and critical strategies of working *with* (codes of conduct, partnerships, certification schemes) and *against* the market (boycotts, shareholder activism, protest and disruption, subvertising) (Newell, 2001). Others go further in trying to confront consumption through voluntary simplicity and living alternative lifestyles, as well as trying to challenge the power and subvert the effect of advertising. Examples include the Transition Network, the anti-consumerist network Enough! and AdBusters, as well as networks such as the Eco-Villages Network. These movements provide an important way of challenging trends towards individualisation of responsibility, commodification, and externalisation and distancing (of consumers from the impacts of their consumption 'choices') (Princen et al., 2002). This is important because, as Maniates argues, 'when responsibility for environmental problems is individualised, there is little room to ponder institutions, the nature and exercise of political power, or ways of collectively changing the distribution of power and influence in society' (2002: 44).

Bringing in New Allies

The depth of behaviour change necessary, at the scale needed to put humanity on a sustainable pathway, means that new allies are needed to facilitate and accelerate shifts and transitions in all aspects of society, with effective coalitions forming around them. This means going beyond the usual suspects (white/ wealthy/middle-class/European/North American, conflict-averse, and more technocratic organisations), and building relationships with immigrant and tenants' rights groups, informal workers, indigenous and racial justice activists. Seeking non-traditional allies who have strong critiques of the status quo and proven capacity to mobilise people and change policies could be a powerful way to scale and deepen change. There is much to learn from grassroots groups whose primary social imperatives successfully achieve environmental goals (Webb et al., 2021), and from unusual alliances unifying diverse groups with common aims to bring about social change, such as waste pickers and middle-class environmental groups in Bangalore, India (Anantharaman, 2014); all of which feeds back into earlier discussions about the need for just transitions and inclusive governance to support social transformation.

Alongside movement allies, there is also scope to engage intermediaries that have profound impacts on consumption pathways and emissions lock-in. A car salesperson who advises a customer to purchase an EV is helping to prevent further emissions lock-in (Sovacool et al., 2020), while estate agents who steer people towards more energy efficient and better insulated properties influence future emissions from housing. Utilising intermediaries is by no means a substitute for public policy interventions, which can be far more targeted, but they provide opportunities to access and shape key junctures and moments of change within our lives. For them to play this role more effectively, different incentive structures around targets and rewards need to be put in place. Other actors may be instrumental as facilitators, influencers, cultural leaders, social guides, intermediaries, and institutional entrepreneurs.

Our behaviours are neither spontaneous nor isolated individual actions as they are intertwined with and shaped by wider economic, political, and cultural structures (Koch, 2019). Culture's undeniable impact on shaping our behaviours makes leveraging the reach and power of cultural leaders essential. Whether they are celebrities, religious leaders, or sports stars, these allies can play a pivotal role in engaging diverse audiences in the process of change. As Westley et al. (2011: 771) suggest in the context of social innovation, 'key persons can play pivotal roles including providing leadership, building trust, developing visions, and sense-making. These individuals can be important brokers for connecting people and networks and also play a key role as nodes in learning networks'.

Reaching out to powerful and influential, yet neglected, sectors with significant scope for behaviour change provides a key lever for scaling change. For instance, in the global sports industry, where travel-related emissions are high, mass catering often unsustainable, waste an issue and advertising revenues from fossil fuel industries (especially airlines) very high, there are a growing number of civil society initiatives emerging. Organisations like Pledgeball, Spirit of Football, and Equal Playing Field are encouraging commitments from fans to change their own behaviour with pledges, as well as putting pressure on their clubs to improve their environmental records. These types of organisations are well placed to tap into the popularity of the sport and the significant media attention it receives to raise the profile of sustainable and equitable lifestyles.

In summary, given the gravity of the situation we face, and the diminishing window of opportunity within which to scale-up action, all options and strategies for change need to be aggressively pursued simultaneously, tailored to the contexts in which they will be enacted. To be successful in creating the social transformations necessary, these must include interventions to bring about *structural* changes to the foundations of our evidently unsustainable economic and political order; intentional changes to transform *systems* – and their management – in relation to infrastructures, institutions, and technologies towards more sustainable lifestyles; and *enabling actors* to organise collectively to achieve a 1.5-degree world. With this in mind, we have sought to emphasise the interdependence and mutually reinforcing nature of strategies directed towards future intervention points, as they can bolster and sustain one another as part of an ecosystem of transformation. We clearly need both individual *and* systemic change. The time for arguing over which comes first has passed. But choices about which combinations of strategies to pursue must be tailored and targeted to the scale and nature of change sought, as well as the context in which they will be pursued. It is clearly also a time for bold experimentation given the scale and severity of the challenge and the potential for positive unforeseen effects as ideas are shared, demands gain traction and unexpected political realignments take place.

In proposing intervention points to initiate these transformational shifts, we need to be mindful that there is clearly significant variance in state capacity, around planning, taxation, enforcement, and the like, as well as different forms of capitalism and state-market relations that undoubtedly shape the nature of leverage points and the scope and likely effectiveness of interventions. This underscores the importance of the more political analysis of behaviour change we have presented in this Element. For instance, what is possible in China might not work in Denmark and vice versa. The degree of engagement from civil society and business is also highly uneven across different political and cultural contexts. Given the different levels of historical responsibility and global interdependence, sectors and regions also have different starting points and baselines from which to shift behaviours. Promoting cycling in the Netherlands has a head start, but it will be harder in the USA because of the size of the country and the design of urban space and dominant cultures around car ownership. Likewise, the baseline for supporting plant-based diets in India, as opposed to in a meat-heavy culture like Argentina, is very different. In many poorer societies there are significant opportunities to avoid lock-in to unsustainable practices altogether and pursue 'lifestyle leapfrogging', supporting these shifts through aid and climate finance. In all societies, however, resistance to change will emerge due to the fact that the most prolific consumers and movers – the polluter elite – are also often the most powerful political actors, using their influence to quash or bypass initiatives that constrain their behaviours. This highlights once more the need for shifts in power relations.

The challenge, therefore, is to identify and activate the virtuous cycles along the spectrum of intervention points, using all levers within the ecosystem of transformation. Insisting on system change as a prerequisite to other types of change discourages and restrains change from below just when we need it the most. This insistence also reifies outdated models of top-down social change that remain popular among some on the Left (encapsulated in the slogan 'one solution, revolution!'), but which fail to account for the fact that individual change can both be a driver for, and a consequence of, systems change (Leventon et al., 2021). Worse still, this insistence can also justify inaction and negate the impacts (positive and negative) we can all have in the multiple roles we fulfil – in the workplace, at home, and as part of communities. Nothing would please fossil fuel companies and multinationals more than the prospect of active citizens being discouraged from taking personal responsibility or mobilising in the everyday, in preference for awaiting the end of capitalism and mass consumerism. At the same time, reducing the challenge to the individualisation of responsibility plays well to those seeking to prevent structural change to an economy in which they are heavily invested and from which they greatly benefit. For this, among other reasons, we need individual *and* system change.

6 Conclusion

The title of this Element is *Changing Our Ways*. We chose the title deliberately to consciously move the debate about behaviour change away from a predominant focus on what individuals and households do in isolation from the economies and societies in which they live and work. There are ways of living and consuming that clearly need to change, starting with the high consumption lifestyles of the richest. There are ways of consuming food and energy that are clearly incompatible with the goals of the Paris Agreement. The ways we meet our needs for mobility, heat and cooling, comfort and security need to be realigned with planetary boundaries. Our ways of working need to transform, possibly working less and certainly working differently to ease the strain on the planet of unsustainable growth and consumerism. Ways of thinking also need to change, though, in order to re-imagine alternatives and disrupt common sense understandings about what is normal, possible, and sustainable. And ways of governing and doing politics need to change. This means intervening to contain and roll-back incumbent power by questioning and reversing the role of money in politics, while also opening new spaces for citizen engagement to help design and pursue a more sustainable future.

We write this Element two years into a devastating global pandemic that has brought about dramatic, but involuntary, behaviour change in patterns of work, mobility, and consumption. But despite early optimism about the potential for this pause in the frenetic pace of life, evidence of the rush to get back to an abnormal 'normal' is there for all to see. From bailouts for oil companies and airlines, to the fast-tracking of controversial infrastructural decisions, and the increased clearing of rainforests in Brazil, for example, many governments have made the most of reduced public scrutiny and scope for social mobilisation to consolidate and advance climate destructive projects. As the Production Gap Report demonstrates, 'G20 governments have directed more COVID-19 recovery support to fossil fuel production and consumption than to renewable energy, energy efficiency, and other low-carbon alternatives (USD 233 billion vs. USD 146 billion, as of November 2020)' (SEI et al., 2020: 20).

Gains in reduced traffic and air travel have been quickly undone. In the case of the United Kingdom, in the first four weeks of the lockdown, carbon emissions fell by 36 per cent. Nevertheless, by June (approximately three months later), Britain's total emissions savings had been reduced to a 16 per cent drop, as more cars returned to its roads, and demand for energy started to rise. Air pollution in China is already back to pre-pandemic levels, with Europe's cities not far behind (CREA, 2020). We are seeing a monumental global resurgence of carbon emissions as economies begin to open up and stimulus money flows into economic activity, with emissions in 2021 soaring by the second highest rate in history (IEA, 2021). We have also seen a rise in single use plastics through the use of masks and protective equipment, which has undone years of work on sustainable behaviour change around plastics and waste. In Britain, we have also witnessed pleas from politicians, notable business people, and the commentariat alike for the public to return to the shops en masse, when safe to do so, as part of their patriotic and civic 'duty' to consume (McKinstry, 2020). These appeals to spend are a tacit acknowledgement that it is only through increased consumption that any type of economic recovery will be secured within the parameters of current economic orthodoxy.

It is also sobering to note that despite unprecedented restrictions on mobility during the pandemic, global emissions fell by only 6.4 per cent in 2020 (Tollefson, 2021), which is less than the carbon reductions of 7.6 per cent required *annually* over the next decade to make a 1.5-degree world possible (UNEP, 2020). Clearly, both those advocating systemic change and behaviour change for sustainability, as well as those keen to bolster their support for incumbents, are seeking to capitalise on the crisis for different ends. Added to this is the fact that responses to the COVID-19 crisis were underpinned by forced behaviour change accompanied (in theory at least) by enforceable sanctions and an agreed and imminent threat, a scenario unlikely to be mirrored in responses to climate change.

Nevertheless, the sense in which today's economy is not fit for the purpose and that for many people, increases in income are not translating into improvements in quality of life, suggests there is an appetite for a more fundamental conversation about sustainable living. We are all on a journey and the final destination is as yet unclear. There are many contradictory road maps about where we might want to get to and how, based on different theories of value and premised on diverse beliefs. We have argued here that, as throughout history, there will be many competing and overlapping pathways to change that seek to navigate the challenge of scaling behaviour change across diverse political, economic, and social contexts characterised by sharp inequalities. We hope to have contributed to an understanding of the politics of this process and the agency different actors have to effect change, in spite of many challenges. Promisingly, we have brought about positive change before and there are at least some positive signs that there is an appetite among a growing number of people to do what is necessary to live differently, but well, on the planet we call home.

Abbreviations

BAU	Business-as-usual
CDR	Carbon Dioxide Removal (technologies)
CSA	Community Supported Agriculture
DTC	Direct to Consumer
EEIOA	Environmentally Extended Input-Output Analysis
EFA	Ecological footprint analysis
EV	Electric Vehicles
GHG	Greenhouse Gas Emissions
IPCC	Intergovernmental Panel on Climate Change
LCA	Life Cycle Analysis
SBC	Sustainable Behaviour Change
SCC	Strong Sustainable Consumption
SCMOs	Sustainable Community Movement Organisations
SDGs	Sustainable Development Goals
SES	Socio-ecological systems
SUV	Sports Utility Vehicle
UNFCCC	United Nations Framework Convention on Climate Change
WSC	Weak Sustainable Consumption

References

Abson, D., Fischer, J., Leventon, J. et al. (2016). 'Leverage points for sustainability transformation'. *Ambio*, 46(1), 30–39.

Adams, M. (2013). 'Inaction and environmental crisis: Narrative, defence mechanisms and the social organisation of denial'. *Psychoanalysis, Culture & Society*, 19(1), 52–71. https://doi.org/10.1057/pcs.2013.21

Adams, M. (2016). *Ecological Crisis, Sustainability and the Psychosocial Subject: Beyond Behaviour Change*. Basingstoke: Palgrave.

Akenji, L. & Chen, H. (2016). *A framework for Shaping Sustainable Lifestyles*. United Nations Environment Programme. www.iges.or.jp/en/publication_docu ments/pub/policyreport/en/5603/-A_framework_for_shaping_sustainable_ lifestyles__determinants_and_strategies-2016Sustainable_lifestyles_FINAL_ not_for_print.pdf.pdf

Akenji, L., Bengtsson, M., Toivio, V. et al. (2021). 1.5-Degree Lifestyles: Towards A Fair Consumption Space for All. Hot or Cool Institute, Berlin. https://hotorcool.org/1-5-degree-lifestyles-report/

Akenji, L., Lettenmeier, M., Koide, R., Toivio, V., & Amellina, A. (2019). 1.5-Degree Lifestyles: Targets and Options for Reducing Lifestyle Carbon Footprints. https://pub.iges.or.jp/pub/15-degrees-lifestyles-2019

Anantharaman, M. (2014). 'Networked ecological citizenship, the new middle classes and the provisioning of sustainable waste management in Bangalore, India'. *Journal Of Cleaner Production*, 63, 173–183. http://doi.org/10.1016/ j.jclepro.2013.08.041

Anantharaman, M. (2018). 'Critical sustainable consumption: a research agenda'. *Journal of Environmental Studies and Sciences*, 8(4), 553–561.

Anderson, K. (2018). Response to the IPCC 1.5°C Special Report [Blog]. http:// blog.policy.manchester.ac.uk/posts/2018/10/response-to-the-ipcc-1-5c-special- report/

Avineri, E. & Goodwin, P. (2010). *Individual Behaviour Change: Evidence in Transport and Public Health*. London: The Department for Transport.

Avolio, B., Walumbwa, F., & Weber, T. (2009). 'Leadership: current theories, research, and future directions'. *Annual Review Of Psychology*, 60(1), 421–449. https://doi.org/10.1146/annurev.psych.60.110707.163621

Bain, P. G., Milfont, T. L., Kashima, Y. et al. (2016). 'Co-benefits of addressing climate change can motivate action around the world'. *Nature Climate Change*, 6(2), 154–157.

Barr, S., Shaw G., Coles T., & Prillwitz J. (2010), '"A holiday is a holiday": practicing sustainability, home and away'. *Journal of Transport Geography*, 18, 474–481.

Bataille, C., Waisman, H., Colombier, M. et al. (2016). The need for national deep decarbonization pathways for effective climate policy. *Climate Policy*, 16(sup1), S7–S26. http://doi.org/10.1080/14693062.2016.1173005

Bauer, M. A., Wilkie, J. E., Kim, J. K., & Bodenhausen, G. V. (2012). 'Cuing consumerism: Situational materialism undermines personal and social well-being'. *Psychological Science*, 23(5), 517–523.

Benanav, A. (2020). *Automation and the Future of Work*. New York: Verso.

Berg, N. & Gigerenzer, G. (2010). 'As-If behavioural economics: neo-classical economics in disguise?' *History of Economic Ideas*, 18(1), 133–165. Retrieved 24 September 2020, from www.jstor.org/stable/23723790

Bernzen, A., Jenkins, J., & Braun, B. (2019). 'Climate change-induced migration in Coastal Bangladesh? A critical assessment of migration drivers in rural households under economic and environmental stress'. *Geosciences*, 9(1), 51. https://doi.org/10.3390/geosciences9010051

Besheer, M. (2020). UN Chief Appeals for Action to Heal 'Broken Planet'. *VOA*. www.voanews.com/science-health/un-chief-appeals-action-heal-broken-planet

Betsill, M, Dubash, N., Paterson, M. et al. (2015). 'Building productive links between the UNFCCC and the broader global climate governance landscape'. *Global Environmental Politics*, 15(2), 1–10.

Bhattacharyya, G. (2018). *Rethinking Racial Capitalism: Questions of Reproduction and Survival*. London: Rowman and Littlefield.

Biermann, F. (2020). 'The future of "environmental" policy in the Anthropocene: time for a paradigm shift'. *Environmental Politics*, 30(1–2), 61–80. http://doi.org/10.1080/09644016.2020.1846958

Biermann, F., Kanie, N., & Kim, R. (2017). 'Global governance by goal-setting: the novel approach of the UN Sustainable Development Goals'. *Current Opinion in Environmental Sustainability*, (26–27), 26–31.

Birney, A. (2021). 'How do we know where there is potential to intervene and leverage impact in a changing system? The practitioners perspective'. *Sustainability Science*, (16), 749–765.

Boardman, B. (2010). *Fixing Fuel Poverty: Challenges and Solutions*. London: Earthscan.

Böhm, S., Jones, C., Land C., & Paterson, M. (eds.). (2006). *Against Automobility*. Oxford: Blackwell.

Bolderdijk, J. W., Steg, L., Geller, E., Lehman, P., & Postmes, T. (2013). 'Comparing the effectiveness of monetary versus moral motives in environmental campaigning'. *Nature Climate Change*, 3, 413–416.

Bollinger, B. & Gillingham, K. (2012). 'Peer effects in the diffusion of solar photovoltaic panels'. *Marketing Science*, 31(6), 900–912. https://doi.org/10.1287/mksc.1120.0727

Borowy, I. & Aillon, J. (2017). 'Sustainable health and degrowth: Health, health care and society beyond the growth paradigm'. *Social Theory & Health*, 15 (3), 346–368. https://doi.org/10.1057/s41285-017-0032-7

Brand, U. & Wissen, M. (2018). 'The imperial mode of living'. In C. Splash (ed.), *Routledge Handbook of Ecological Economics: Nature and Society*. Abingdon: Routledge, pp. 152–161.

Brand, U. & Wissen, M. (2021). *The Imperial Mode of Living: Everyday Life and the Ecological Crisis of Capitalism* (pp. 1–256). London: Verso.

Bulkeley, H. (2016). *Accomplishing Climate Governance* Cambridge: Cambridge University Press.

Bulkeley, H., Andonva, L., Betsill, M. M. et al. (2014). *Transnational Climate Change Governance* Cambridge: Cambridge University Press.

Burningham, K. & Venn, S. (2017). 'Are lifecourse transitions opportunities for moving to more sustainable consumption?'. *Journal Of Consumer Culture*, 20(1), 102–121. http://doi.org/10.1177/1469540517729010

Burger, A. (2015). *Extreme Working Hours in Western Europe and North America: A New Aspect of Polarization*. LSE 'Europe in Question', Discussion Paper Series.

Cabinet Office Behavioural Insights Team/DECC/DCL. (2011). Behaviour Change and Energy Use. Crown copyright. https://www.gov.uk/government/publications/behaviour-change-and-energy-use-behavioural-insights-team-paper

Cafaro, P. (2011). 'Beyond business as usual: alternative wedges to avoid catastrophic climate change and create sustainable societies'. Arnold, D. (ed) *The Ethics of Global Climate Change*, Cambridge: Cambridge University Press, 192–215.

Cameron R., Geels, F. W., Lockwood, M. et al. (2018). 'The politics of accelerating low-carbon transitions: Towards a new research agenda', *Energy Research & Social Science*, 44, 304–311.

Capstick, S., Lorenzoni, I., Corner, A., & Whitmarsh, L. (2015). 'Prospects for radical emissions reduction through behavior and lifestyle change'. *Carbon management*, 5(4), 429–445.

Carbon, T. (2020). 'Groundhog Pay: How Executive Incentives Trap Companies in a Loop of Fossil Growth'. *Carbon Tracker*. https://carbon

tracker.org/reports/groundhog-pay-how-executive-incentives-trap-compan
ies-in-a-loop-of-fossil-growth/

Carlson, A. E. (2005). 'Social norms and individual environmental behavior'. *Environmental Law Reporter. News & Analysis*, 35, 10763.

Centola, D., Becker, J., Brackbill, D., & Baronchelli, A. (2018). 'Experimental evidence for tipping points in social convention'. *Science*, 360(6393), 1116–1119.

Chenoweth, E. & Stephan, M. (2011). *Why Civil Resistance Works: The Strategic Logic of Nonviolent Conflict*. New York: Columbia University Press.

Citizen Assembly UK. (2020). The Path to Net Zero: Climate Assembly UK Full Report. www.climateassembly.uk/report/

Clapp, J. & Dauvergne, P. (2011). *Paths to a Green World: The Political Economy of the Global Environment* (2nd ed.). [S.l.]: The MIT Press.

Clarke, J., Corner, A., & Webster, R. (2018). *Public Engagement for a 1.5C World – Shifting Gear and Scaling up*. Retrieved 31 March 2019, from Climate Outreach website: https://climateoutreach.org/resources/public-engagement-1-5c-ipcc-sr15/

Cohen, M. (2019). 'From work time reduction to a post-work future: Implications for sustainable consumption governance' in Mont, O. (ed) *A Research Agenda For Sustainable Consumption Governance*, Cheltenham: Edward Elgar, 185–200.

Contessi, S. & Li, L. (2013). *Translating Kurzarbeit*. Economic Synopses. Federal Reserve Bank of St. Louis.

Convention Citoyenne pour le Climat. (2020). *Les Propositions de la Convention Citoyenne pour le Climat, Thématique: se déplacer*. Paris. https://propositions.conventioncitoyennepourleclimat.fr/pdf/ccc-rapportf inal-sedeplacer.pdf.

CREA. (2020). '*Air pollution returns to European capitals: Paris faces largest rebound*'. https://energyandcleanair.org/pollution-returns-to-european-capitals/

CSO Equity Review. (2018). *After Paris: Inequality, Fair Shares, and the Climate Emergency*. Manila, London, Cape Town, Washington, et al.: CSO Equity Review Coalition. [civilsocietyreview.org/report2018]

D'Alisa, G., Demaria, F., & Kallis, G. (2015). *Degrowth*. Abingdon: Routledge.

Darnton, A., Verplanken, B., White, P., & Whitmarsh, L. (2011). Habits, routines and sustainable lifestyles: A summary report to the Department for Environment, Food and Rural Affairs. *AD Research & Analysis for Defra*, London.

Dauvergne, P. (2008). *The Shadows of Consumption: Consequences for the Global Environment*. Cambridge: MIT Press.

Davelaar, D. (2021). 'Transformation for sustainability: a deep leverage points approach'. *Sustainability Science*, 16, 727–747.

DEFRA (2008). *A Framework for Pro-environmental Behaviours*, Report by the UK Department for Environment, Food and Rural Affairs. Defra: London.

De Moor, J. & Verhaegen, S. (2020). 'Gateway or getaway? Testing the link between lifestyle politics and other modes of political participation'. *European Political Science Review*, 12(1), 91–111.

Devaney, L., Torney, D., Brereton, P., & Coleman, M. (2020). 'Ireland's citizens' assembly on climate change: Lessons for deliberative public engagement and communication'. *Environmental Communication*, 14(2), 141–146. https://doi.org/10.1080/17524032.2019.1708429

Dietz, T., Gardner, G. T., Gilligan, J., Stern, P. C., & Vandenbergh, M. P. (2009). 'Household actions can provide a behavioral wedge to rapidly reduce US carbon emissions'. *Proceedings of the National Academy of Sciences*, 106 (44), 18452–18456.

Dietz, T., Shwom, R. L., & Whitley, C. T. (2020). 'Climate change and society'. *Annual Review of Sociology*, 46(1), 135–158.

Di Guilio, A. & Fuchs, D. (2014). 'Sustainable consumption corridors: Concept, objections, and responses'. *GAIA*, 23/S1, 184–192.

Doherty, K. L. & Webler, T. N. (2016). 'Social norms and efficacy beliefs drive the Alarmed segment's public sphere climate actions'. *Nature Climate Change*, 6, 879–884.

Dolan, P., Hallsworth, M., Halpern, D. et al. (2012). 'Influencing behaviour: The mindspace way'. *Journal Of Economic Psychology*, 33(1), 264–277. https://doi.org/10.1016/j.joep.2011.10.009

Dorling, D. (2017). 'Is inequality bad for the environment?'. *The Guardian*. July 4th: www.theguardian.com/inequality/2017/jul/04/is-inequality-bad-for-the-environment.

Drawdown Project (2020). www.leonardodicaprio.org/project-drawdown-100-solutions-to-reverse-global-warming/ Accessed 21 July 2020.

Dryzek, J. & Niemeyer, S. (2019). 'Deliberative democracy and climate governance'. *Nature Human Behaviour*, 3(5), 411–413. http://doi.org/10.1038/s41562-019-0591-9

Dubois, G., Sovacool, B., Aall, C. et al. (2019). 'It starts at home? Climate policies targeting household consumption and behavioral decisions are key to low-carbon futures'. *Energy Research & Social Science*, 52, 144–158.

Elliott, L. (2020). 'Four-day week would be affordable for most UK firms, says thinktank'. *The Guardian*. Retrieved 2 January 2021, from www .theguardian.com/business/2020/dec/29/four-day-week-would-be-afford able-for-most-uk-firms-says-thinktank.

Evans, D. M. (2019). 'What is consumption, where has it been going, and does it still matter?' *The Sociological Review*, 67(3), 499–517.

Evans, D. & Jackson, T. (2008). 'Sustainable consumption: Perspectives from social and cultural theory'. *RESOLVE Working Paper* 05-08, Guildford: University of Surrey.

Evans, D., McMeekin, A., & Southerton, D. (2012). 'Sustainable consumption, behaviour change policies and theories of practice'. In A. Warde & D. Southerton (eds.), *The Habits of Consumption*. Studies across Disciplines in the Humanities and Social Sciences 12. Helsinki: Helsinki Collegium for Advanced Studies, 113–129.

Fitzgerald, J., Schor, J., & Jorgenson, A. (2018). 'Working hours and carbon dioxide emissions in the United States 2007-2013'. *Social Forces*, 64(4), 1851–1874.

Food and Agriculture Organization of the United Nations [FAO]. (2011). *Global Food Losses and Food Waste – Extent, Causes and Prevention*. Rome: FAO.

Food and Agriculture Organization of the United Nations [FAO]. (2019). *The State of Food and Agriculture 2019. Moving Forward on Food Loss and Waste Reduction*. Rome: FAO.

Food and Agriculture Organization of the United Nations [FAO]. (2020). *Global food markets still brace for uncertainty in 2020/21 because of COVID-19 says FAO*. www.fao.org/news/story/en/item/1287515/icode/

Forno, F. & Graziano, P. (2014). 'Sustainable community movement organisations'. *Journal Of Consumer Culture*, 14(2), 139–157. https://doi .org/10.1177/1469540514526225

Fouquet, R. (2016). 'Historical energy transitions: Speed, prices and system transformation'. *Energy Research and Social Science*, 22, 7–12.

Frank, R. H. (2020). *Under the Influence: Putting Peer Pressure to Work*. Princeton New Jersey: Princeton University Press.

Fuchs, D. & Lorek, S. (2005) 'Sustainable consumption governance. A history of promises and failures'. *Journal of Consumer Policy*, 28(3), 261–288.

Fuchs, D., Lorek, S., Di Giulio, A., & Defila, R. (2019). 'Sources of power for sustainable consumption: Where to look'. In M. Martiskainen, L. Middlemiss & C. Isenhour (eds.). *Power and Politics in Sustainable Consumption Research and Practice*. London: Routledge, 62–83.

Fuchs, D., Di Giulio, A., Glaab, K. et al. (2016). 'Power: The missing element in sustainable consumption and absolute reductions research and action'. *Journal of Cleaner Production*, 132, 298–307.

Fuchs, D., Sahakian, M., Gumbert, T. et al. (2021). *Consumption Corridors: Living a Good Life within Sustainable Limits*. New York: Routledge.

Gaventa, J. (2006). 'Finding the spaces for change: a power analysis'. *IDS Bulletin*, 37(6), 23–33.

Gächter, S. & Renner, E. (2018). 'Leaders as role models and "belief managers" in social dilemmas'. *Journal of Economic Behavior & Organization*, 154, 321–334.

GDR. (2018). 'Greenhouse Development Rights', http://gdrights.org/.

Geels, F. (2014). 'Regime resistance against low-carbon transitions: Introducing politics and power into the multi-level perspective'. *Theory, Culture & Society*, 31(5), 21–40. http://doi.org/10.1177/0263276414531627

Geels, F. (2005). *Technological Transitions and System Innovations: A Co-Evolutionary and Socio-Technical Analysis*. Cheltenham: Edward Elgar.

Geels, F., Sovacool, B., Schwanen, T., & Sorrell, S. (2017). 'The socio-technical dynamics of low-carbon transitions'. *Joule*, 1(3), 463–479.

Giddens A. (1991). *Modernity and Self-Identity*. Stanford: Stanford University Press.

Girod, B., van Vuuren, D. P., & Hertwich, E. G. (2014). 'Climate policy through changing consumption choices: Options and obstacles for reducing greenhouse gas emissions'. *Global Environmental Change*, 25, 5–15.

Global Commons Institute [GCI]. (2018). 'Contraction and Convergence', http://gci.org.uk/

Gomez-Zavaglia, A., Mejuto, J., & Simal-Gandara, J. (2020). 'Mitigation of emerging implications of climate change on food production systems'. *Food Research International*, 134, 109256. https://doi.org/10.1016/j.foodres .2020.109256

Goodwin, T. (2012). Why we should reject 'nudge'. *Politics*, 32(2), 85–92. https://doi.org/10.1111/j.1467-9256.2012.01430.x

Gore, T. & Alestig, M. (2020). *Confronting Carbon Inequality in the European Union: Why the European Green Deal must Tackle Inequality While Cutting Emissions*. Oxford: Oxfam. www.oxfam.org/en/research/confronting-car bon-inequality-european-union

Green, F. (2018). 'Anti-fossil fuel norms'. *Climatic Change*, 150(1–2), 103–116. https://doi.org/10.1007/s10584-017-2134-6

Green, F. & Dennis, R. (2018). 'Cutting with both arms of the scissors: The economic and political case for restrictive supply-side climate policies'. *Climatic Change*, 150(1–2), 73–87.

Grubler, A., Wilson, C., Bento, N. et al. (2018). 'A low energy demand scenario for meeting the 1.5 °C target and sustainable development goals without negative emission technologies'. *Nature Energy*, 3(6), 515.

Haberl, H., Wiedenhofer, D., Virág, D. et al. (2020). 'A systematic review of the evidence on decoupling of GDP, resource use and GHG emissions, part II: synthesizing the insights'. *Environmental Research Letters*, 15(6), 065003.

Hale, T. (2016). 'All hands on deck: the Paris Agreement and non-state climate action'. *Global Environmental Politics*, 16(3), 12–21.

Hall, P. (1993). 'Policy paradigms, social learning and the state: The case of economic policymaking in Britain'. *Comparative Politics*, 25(3), 275–296. https://doi.org/10.2307/422246

Hardman, S., Chandan, A., Tal, G., & Turrentine, T. (2017). 'The effectiveness of financial purchase incentives for battery electric vehicles–A review of the evidence'. *Renewable and Sustainable Energy Reviews*, 80, 1100–1111.

Heglar, M. (2019). 'I work in the environmental movement. I don't care if you recycle'. Vox. Retrieved 25 September 2020, from www.vox.com/the-high light/2019/5/28/18629833/climate-change-2019-green-new-deal.

Hertwich, E. G. & Peters, G. (2009). 'Carbon footprint of nations: A global, trade-linked analysis'. *Environmental Science & Technology*, 43(16), 6414–6420.

Hickel, J. (2019). 'Is it possible to achieve a good life for all within planetary boundaries?' *Third World Quarterly*, 40(1), 18–35.

Hickel, J. (2020). *Less is More: How Degrowth will Save the World*. London: William Heinemann.

Hiteva, R. & Sovacool, B. (2017). 'Harnessing social innovation for energy justice: A business model perspective'. *Energy Policy*, 107, 631–639. https://doi.org/10.1016/j.enpol.2017.03.056

Hooper, K., Fellingham, L., Clancy, J., Newell, P., & Petrova, S. (2021). *Gender Race and Social Inclusion – Net Zero Transitions: A Review of the Literature*, Department of Business, Energy and Industrial Strategy, December 2021.

Hopkins, R. (2019). *From What Is to What If: Unleashing the Power of Imagination to Create the Future We Want*. London: Chelsea Green.

Howell, R. & Allen, S. (2017). 'People and planet: Values, motivations and formative influences of individuals acting to mitigate climate change'. *Environmental Values*, 26(2), 131–155. https://doi.org/10.3197/09632711 7x14847335385436

Howell, R., Capstick, S., & Whitmarsh, L. (2016). 'Impacts of adaptation and responsibility framings on attitudes towards climate change mitigation'. *Climatic Change*, 136(3–4), 445–461. https://doi.org/10.1007/s10584-016-1627-z

Huber, M. (2021). 'Rich people are fueling climate catastrophe – But not mostly because of their consumption'. *Jacobin*. https://jacobinmag.com/2021/05/rich-people-climate-change-consumption

IEA. (2020). *World Energy Outlook 2020*. Paris: IEA. www.iea.org/reports/world-energy-outlook-2020

IEA. (2021). *Global Energy Review 2021*. Paris: IEA. www.iea.org/reports/global-energy-review-2021

International Labour Office [ILO] (2018). *Care Work and Care Jobs for the Future of Decent Work*. Geneva: ILO.

IPCC. (2018). Summary for Policymakers. In: Global Warming of 1.5°C. An IPCC Special Report on the impacts of global warming of 1.5°C above pre-industrial levels and related global greenhouse gas emission pathways, in the context of strengthening the global response to the threat of climate change, sustainable development, and efforts to eradicate poverty [Masson-Delmotte, V., P. Zhai, H.-O. Pörtner, D. Roberts, J. Skea, P.R. Shukla, A. Pirani, W. Moufouma-Okia, C. Péan, R. Pidcock, S. Connors, J.B.R. Matthews, Y. Chen, X. Zhou, M.I. Gomis, E. Lonnoy, T. Maycock, M. Tignor, and T. Waterfield (eds.)].

Ivanova, D., Barrett, J., Wiedenhofer, D. et al. (2020). 'Quantifying the potential for climate change mitigation of consumption options'. *Environmental Research Letters*, 15(9), 093001.

Jackson, T. (2005). 'Motivating sustainable consumption: A review of evidence on consumer behaviour and behavioural change'. *Sustainable Development Research Network*, 29, 30.

Jackson, T. (2006). *The Earthscan Reader in Sustainable Consumption*. London: Earthscan.

Jackson, T. (2011). *Prosperity without Growth: Economics for a Finite Planet*. London: Earthscan.

Jackson, T. (2021). *Post-Growth: Life after Capitalism*. Cambridge: Polity.

Jackson, T., Burningham, K., Catney, P. et al. (2016). Understanding sustainable prosperity – Towards a transdisciplinary research agenda. *CUSP Working Paper Series*, No 1. Centre for the Understanding of Sustainable Prosperity, Guildford: University of Surrey.

Jessop, B. (2010). 'Cultural political economy and critical policy studies'. *Critical Policy Studies*, 3(3–4), 336–356.

Jiren, T., Riechers, M., Bergsten, A., & Fischer, J. (2021). 'A leverage points perspective on institutions for food security in a smallholder-dominated landscape in southwestern Ethiopia'. *Sustainability Science*, 16(3), 767–779. http://doi.org/10.1007/s11625-021-00936-9

John, P., Cotterill, S., Moseley, A. et al. (2013). *Nudge, Nudge, Think, Think: Experimenting with Ways to Change Civic Behaviour.* London: Bloomsbury Academic.

Johnson, O., Yi Chen Han, J., Knight, A. et al. (2020). 'Intersectionality and energy transitions: A review of gender, social equity and low-carbon energy'. *Energy Research and Social Science*, 70 (February), 101774. http://doi.org/10.1016/j.erss.2020.101774.

Jones, R., Pykett, J., & Whitehead, M. (2011). 'The geographies of soft paternalism in the UK: the rise of the avuncular state and changing behaviour after neoliberalism'. *Geography Compass*, 5(1), 50–62.

Jordan, A., Huitema, D., Van Asselt, H., & Forster, J. (eds.). (2018). *Governing Climate Change: Polycentricity in Action?* Cambridge: Cambridge University Press.

Kalaniemi, S., Ottelin, J., Heinonen, J., & Junnila, S. (2020). 'Downscaling consumption to universal basic income level falls short of sustainable carbon footprint in Finland'. *Environmental Science & Policy*, 114, 377–383. https://doi.org/10.1016/j.envsci.2020.09.006

Kallis, G., Paulson, S., D'Alisa, G., & Demaria, F. (2020). *The Case for Degrowth.* Cambridge: John Wiley & Sons.

Kalmus, P. (2017). *Being the Change: Live Well and Spark a Climate Revolution.* Grabiola Island Canada: New Society Publishers.

Kartha, S., Kemp-Benedict, E., Ghosh, E., Nazareth, A., & Gore, T. (2020). *The Carbon Inequality Era: An assessment of the global distribution of consumption emissions among individuals from 1990 to 2015 and beyond.* Joint Research Report. Stockholm Environment Institute and Oxfam International.

Kasser, T. (2002). *The High Price of Materialism.* Cambridge: MIT Press.

Kasser, T. (2016). 'Materialistic values and goals'. *Annual Review of Psychology*, 67, 489–514.

Kasser, T. & Sheldon, K. M. (2009). 'Time affluence as a path toward personal happiness and ethical business practice: Empirical evidence from four studies'. *Journal of Business Ethics*, 84(2), 243–255.

Kenner, D. (2019). *Carbon Inequality: The Role of the Richest in Climate Change.* Abingdon: Routledge.

Keyßer, L. & Lenzen, M. (2021). '1.5 °C degrowth scenarios suggest the need for new mitigation pathways'. *Nature Communications*, 12(1). http://doi.org/10.1038/s41467-021-22884-9

Knight, K., Rosa, E., & Schor, J. (2013). 'Could working less reduce pressures on the environment? A cross-national panel analysis of OECD countries, 1970–2007'. *Global Environmental Change*, 23(4), 691–700. https://doi.org/10.1016/j.gloenvcha.2013.02.017

Koch, M. (2019). 'Growth strategies and consumption patterns in transition: From Fordism to finance-driven capitalism' in Mont, O. (ed) *A Research Agenda For Sustainable Consumption Governance*, Cheltenham: Edward Elgar, 35–49. https://doi.org/10.4337/9781788117814.00011

Kollmuss, A. & Agyeman, J. (2002). 'Mind the gap: Why do people act environmentally and what are the barriers to pro-environmental behavior?' *Environmental Education Research*, 8(3), 239–260.

KR Rapid Transition Task Force. (2019). *Making Change Happen: Foundations for Intervening to Achieve Rapid Sustainable Behaviour Change*. Internal report for KR foundation.

Kraft-Todd, G. T., Bollinger, B., Gillingham, K., Lamp, S., & Rand, D. G. (2018). 'Credibility-enhancing displays promote the provision of non-normative public goods'. *Nature*, 563(7730), 245.

Krasner, S. (1983). (ed.). *International Regimes*. Itacha: Cornell University Press.

Kuhnhenn, K. (2018). *Economic Growth in Mitigation Scenarios: A Blind Spot in Climate Science*. Berlin: Heinrich Böll Stiftung. www.boell.de/sites/default/files/endf2_kuhnhenn_growth_in_mitigation_scenarios.pdf

Kythreotis, A., Mantyka-Pringle, C., Mercer, T. et al. (2019). 'Citizen social science for more integrative and effective climate action: A science-policy perspective'. *Frontiers In Environmental Science*, 7: 1–10. https://doi.org/10.3389/fenvs.2019.00010

Lam, D. P. M., Martín-López, B., Wiek, A., Bennett, E. M., Frantzeskaki, N., Horcea-Milcu, A. I., & Lang, D. J. (2020). 'Scaling the impact of sustainability initiatives: A typology of amplification processes. *Urban Transformations*, 3(2). https://doi.org/10.1186/s42854-020-00007-9

Lawhon, M. & McCreary, T. (2020). 'Beyond jobs vs environment: On the potential of universal basic income to reconfigure environmental politics'. *Antipode*, 52(2), 452–474. https://doi.org/10.1111/anti.12604

Lawrence, M., Buller, A., Baines, J., & Hager, S. (2020). *Commoning the Company*. Common Wealth. www.common-wealth.co.uk/reports/commoning-the-company

Lehner, M., Mont, O., & Heiskanen, E. (2016). 'Nudging – A promising tool for sustainable consumption behaviour?' *Journal of Cleaner Production*, 134, 166–177.

Leiserowitz, A. (2019). 'Building public and political will for climate action'. In Esty, D. (ed.), *A Better Planet: 37 Big Ideas for a Sustainable Future*. New Haven: Yale University Press.

Lenton, T. M. & Williams, H. T. P. (2013). 'On the origin of planetary-scale tipping points'. *Trends in Ecololgy & Evolution*. 28, 380–382.

Lertzman, R. (2014). *Psychosocial contributions to climate sciences communications research and practice*, Ph.D Overview.

Leventon, J., Abson, D., & Lang, D. (2021). 'Leverage points for sustainability transformations: nine guiding questions for sustainability science and practice'. *Sustainability Science*, 16(3), 721–726. http://doi.org/10.1007/s11625-021-00961-8

Liefferink, D. & Wurzel, R. K. (2017). 'Environmental leaders and pioneers: agents of change?' *Journal of European Public Policy*, 24(7), 951–968.

Linnér, B. O. & Wibeck, V. (2021). 'Drivers of sustainability transformations: leverage points, contexts and conjunctures'. *Sustainability Science*, 16, 889–900.

Lorek, S. & Fuchs, D. (2013). 'Strong sustainable consumption governance: a precondition for a degrowth path?' *Journal of Cleaner Production*, 38, 36–43.

Lorenzoni, I., Nicholson-Cole, S., & Whitmarsh, L. (2007). 'Barriers perceived to engaging with climate change among the UK public and their policy implications'. *Global Environmental Change*, 17(3–4), 445–459. http://doi.org/10.1016/j.gloenvcha.2007.01.004

Lukes, S. (1974). *Power: A Radical View*. London: Macmillan.

Maniates, M. (2001). 'Individualization: Plant a tree, buy a bike, save the world?' *Global Environmental Politics*, 1(3): 31–52.

Maniates, M. (2002). 'In search of consumptive resistance: The voluntary simplicity movement'. In Princen, T., Maniates, M. and Conca, K. (eds) *Confronting Consumption* Cambridge MA: MIT Press, 199–236.

Mao, C., Koide, R., & Akenji, L. (2020). 'Applying foresight to policy design for a long-term transition to sustainable lifestyles'. *Sustainability*, 12, 6200.

Mattioli, G., Roberts, C., Steinberger, J., & Brown, A. (2020). 'The political economy of car dependence: A systems of provision approach'. *Energy Research & Social Science*, 66, 101486. https://doi.org/10.1016/j.erss.2020.101486.

McKinstry, L. (2020). It is your patriotic duty to spend spend spend on the high street. *The Daily Express*. www.express.co.uk/comment/columnists/leo-mckinstry/1304105/coronavirus-economy-spend-high-street-money-saved

McLoughlin, N., Corner, A., Clarke, J. et al. (2019). *Mainstreaming Low-carbon Lifestyles*. Climate Outreach & CASPI. https://talk.eco/wp-content/uploads/Climate-Outreach-CASPI-Mainstreaming-low-carbon-lifestyles.pdf

Meadows, D. (1999). *Leverage Points: Places to Intervene in a System*. Hartland: The Sustainability Institute.

Millward-Hopkins, J. & Oswald, Y. (2021). '"Fair" inequality, consumption and climate mitigation'. *Environmental Research Letters*, 16 (3): 1–10.

Millward-Hopkins, J., Steinberger, J., Rao, N., & Oswald, Y. (2020). 'Providing decent living with minimum energy: A global scenario'. *Global Environmental Change*, 65, 102168. https://doi.org/10.1016/j.gloenvcha.2020.102168

Moberg, K. R., Aall, C., Dorner, F. et al. (2019). 'Mobility, food and housing: responsibility, individual consumption and demand-side policies in European deep decarbonisation pathways'. *Energy Efficiency* 12, 497–519.

Momsen, K. & Stoerk, T. (2014). 'From intention to action: Can nudges help consumers to choose renewable energy?'. *Energy Policy*, 74, 376–382. https://doi.org/10.1016/j.enpol.2014.07.008

Moore, J. (2015). 'Ecological footprints and lifestyle archetypes: Exploring dimensions of consumption and the transformation needed to achieve urban sustainability'. *Sustainability*, 7(4), 4747–4763.

Muradova, L., Walker, H., & Colli, F. (2020). 'Climate change communication and public engagement in interpersonal deliberative settings: evidence from the Irish citizens' assembly'. *Climate Policy*, 20(10), 1322–1335. https://doi.org/10.1080/14693062.2020.1777928

Nash, N., Whitmarsh, L., Capstick, S. et al. (2017). 'Climate-relevant behavioral spillover and the potential contribution of social practice theory'. *Wiley Interdisciplinary Reviews: Climate Change*, 8(6), e481.

Nature Human Behaviour (2020). 'Nudges that don't nudge'. Editorial 18.02.2020. 4, 121. https://doi.org/10.1038/s41562-020-0832-y

New Economics Foundation [NEF]. (2016). *The Happy Planet Index 2016: A Global Index of Sustainable Wellbeing*. London: NEF.

Newell, P. (2001). 'Managing multinationals: The governance of investment for the environment'. *Journal of International Development*, 13, 907–919.

Newell, P. (2005). 'Race, class and the global politics of environmental inequality'. *Global Environmental Politics*, 5(3), 70–94.

Newell, P. (2018). 'Trasformismo or transformation? The global political economy of energy transitions'. *Review of International Political Economy*, 26(1), 25–48.

Newell, P. (2020). 'Race and the politics of energy transitions'. *Energy Research and Social Science*, 71.

Newell, P. (2021). *Power Shift: The Global Political Economy of Energy Transitions*. Cambridge: Cambridge University Press.

Newell, P. & Martin, A. (2020). *The Role of the State in the Politics of Disruption & Acceleration*. London: Climate KIC.

Newell, P. & Simms, A. (2019). 'Towards a fossil fuel non-proliferation treaty'. *Climate Policy*, 20(8), 1043–1054.

Newell, P. & Simms, A. (2020). 'How did we do that? Histories and political economies of rapid and just transitions'. *New Political Economy*, 26 (6): 907–922. http://doi.org/10.1080/13563467.2020.1810216

Newell, P., Bulkeley, H., Turner, K. et al. (2015). 'Governance traps in climate change politics: re-framing the debate in terms of responsibilities and rights'. *Wiley Interdisciplinary Reviews: Climate Change*, 6(6), 535–540.

Newell, P., Daley, F., & Twena, M. (2021). *Changing our ways? Behaviour change and the climate crisis*. Report of the Cambridge Sustainability Commission on Scaling Behaviour Change.

Newell, P., Twena, M., & Daley, F. (2021a). 'Scaling behaviour change for a 1.5 degree world: Challenges and opportunities'. *Global Sustainability*, 4(e22), 1–13. https://doi.org/10.1017/sus.2021.23.

Nielsen, K. S., Clayton, S., Stern, P. C. et al. (2020). 'How psychology can help limit climate change'. *American Psychologist*. 76(1): 130–144.

Nielsen, K. S., Nicholas, K. A., Creutzig, F., Dietz, T., & Stern, P. C., (2021). 'The role of high-socioeconomic-status people in locking in or rapidly reducing energy-driven greenhouse gas emissions'. *Nature Energy*, 2021, 1–6. https://doi.org/10.1038/s41560-021-00900-y

Nikiforuk, A. (2021). *The Energy of Slaves: Oil and the New Servitude*. Vancouver: Greystone Books.

Nisa, C. F., Bélanger, J. J., Schumpe, B. M., & Faller, D. G. (2019). 'Meta-analysis of randomised controlled trials testing behavioural interventions to promote household action on climate change'. *Nature Communications*, 10(1), 1–13.

O'Brien, K., Reams, J., Caspari, A. et al. (2013). 'You say you want a revolution? Transforming education and capacity building in response to global change'. *Environmental Science & Policy*, 28, 48–59. https://doi.org/10.1016/j.envsci.2012.11.011

O'Brien, K. & Sygna, L. (2013). 'Responding to climate change: the three spheres of transformation'. *Proceedings of Transformation in a Changing Climate*, 16, 23.

O'Neill, D., Fanning, A., Lamb, W., & Steinberger, J. (2018). 'A good life for all within planetary boundaries'. *Nature Sustainability*, 1(2), 88–95. http://doi.org/10.1038/s41893-018-0021-4

Ostrom, E. (2010). 'Polycentric systems for coping with collective action and global environmental change'. *Global Environmental Change*, 20(4), 550–557.

Otto, I. M., Donges, J. F., Cremades, R. et al. (2020). 'Social tipping dynamics for stabilizing Earth's climate by 2050'. *Proceedings of the National Academy of Sciences*, 117(5), 2354–2365.

Otto, I. M., Donges, J. F., Lucht, W., & Schellnhuber, H. J. (2020a). 'Reply to Smith et al.: Social tipping dynamics in a world constrained by conflicting interests'. *Proceedings of the National Academy of Sciences,* 2020, 202002648. https://doi.org/10.1073/pnas.2002648117

Otto, I., Kim, K., Dubrovsky, N., & Lucht, W. (2019). 'Shift the focus from the super-poor to the super-rich'. *Nature Climate Change,* 9(2), 82–84. https://doi.org/10.1038/s41558-019-0402-3

Patel, R. & Moore, J. (2018). *A History of the World in Seven Cheap Things.* London: Verso.

Paterson, M. (2006). *Automobile Politics.* Cambridge: Cambridge University Press.

Paterson, M., Hoffman, M., Betsill, M., & Bernstein, S. (2014). 'The micro foundations of policy diffusion toward complex global governance: An analysis of the transnational carbon emission trading network'. *Comparative Political Studies,* 47(3), 420–449.

Patterson, J., Thaler, T., Hoffmann, M. et al. (2018). 'Political feasibility of 1.5° C societal transformations: the role of social justice'. *Current Opinion in Environmental Sustainability,* 31, 1–9. http://doi.org/10.1016/j.cosust.2017.11.002

Pega, F., Náfrádi, B., Momen, N. et al. (2021). 'Global, regional, and national burdens of ischemic heart disease and stroke attributable to exposure to long working hours for 194 countries, 2000–2016: A systematic analysis from the WHO/ILO joint estimates of the work-related burden of disease and injury'. *Environment International,* 106595. http://doi.org/10.1016/j.envint.2021.106595

Petridou, E. & Mintrom, M. (2020). 'A research agenda for the study of policy entrepreneurs'. *Policy Studies Journal.* 49(4): 943–68 http://doi.org/10.1111/psj.12405

Perkins, P. (2019). 'Climate justice, commons, and degrowth'. *Ecological Economics,* 160, 183–190. https://doi.org/10.1016/j.ecolecon.2019.02.005

Piguet, E. & Laczko, F. (2014). (eds.) *People on the move in a changing climate: The Regional Impact of Environmental Change on Migration.* Netherlands: SpringerLink.

Piketty, T. (2014). *Capital in the Twenty-First Century.* Padstow: TJ International.

Princen, T. (2005). *The Logic of Sufficiency.* Cambridge: MIT Press.

Princen, T., Maniates, M., & Conca, K. (2002). (eds.) *Confronting Consumption,* Cambridge: MIT Press.

Raworth, K. (2017). *Doughnut Economics: Seven Ways to Think Like a 21st-Century Economist.* New York: Random House Business Books.

Raworth, K. et al. (2020). *The Amsterdam City Doughnut: A Tool for Transformative Action.* Amsterdam: City of Amsterdam.

Rees, W. & Moore, J. (2013). 'Ecological footprints, fair earth-shares and urbanization'. In R. Vale & B. Vale (eds.), *Living within a Fair Share Ecological Footprint.* Abingdon: Routledge, 3–33.

RESET. (2020). 'Time to Reset: The public desire for a fairer, greener Britain after Covid'. *All Parliamentary Group on the Green New Deal.* https://reset-uk.org/static/TimeToReset-3a6ee92ce4fff64d024c62404f53fe5c.pdf

Rinkinen, J., Shove, E., & Torriti, J. (eds.). (2019). *Energy Fables: Challenging Ideas in the Energy Sector.* Abingdon: Routledge.

Roberts, J. T. & Parks, B. C. (2008). 'Fuelling injustice: globalization, ecologically unequal exchange and climate change'. In J. Ooshthoek and B. Gills (eds.), *The Globalization of Environmental Crises.* London: Routledge, 169–187.

Rosnick, D. & Weisbrot, M. (2007). 'Are shorter work hours good for the environment? A comparison of US and European energy consumption'. *International Journal of Health Services*, 37(3), 405–417.

Royston, S., Selby, J., & Shove, E. (2018). 'Invisible energy policies: A new agenda for energy demand reduction'. *Energy Policy*, 123, 127–135.

Sanne, C. (2002). 'Willing consumers – or locked-in? Policies for a sustainable consumption'. *Ecological Economics*, 42(1–2), 273–287.

Schmidt, V. A. (2013). 'Democracy and legitimacy in the European Union revisited: Input, output and "throughput"'. *Political Studies*, 61(1), 2–22.

Schor, J. (2011). *True Wealth: How and Why Millions of Americans Are Creating a Time-Rich, Ecologically Light, Small-Scale, High-Satisfaction Economy.* New York: Penguin Books.

Schor, J. (2015). 'Climate, inequality, and the need for reframing climate policy'. *Review of Radical Political Economics*, 47(4), 525–536.

Schlaile, M., Urmetzer, S., Ehrenberger, M., & Brewer, J. (2020). 'Systems entrepreneurship: a conceptual substantiation of a novel entrepreneurial "species"'. *Sustainability Science*, 16(3), 781–794. http://doi.org/10.1007/s11625-020-00850-6

Schroeder, P. & Anantharaman, M. (2017). '"Lifestyle leapfrogging" in emerging economies: Enabling systemic shifts to sustainable consumption'. *Journal of Consumer Policy*, 40(1), 3–23.

Schumacher, E. (1973). *Small is Beautiful: A Study of Economics As If People Mattered.* London: Abacus.

Scoones, I., Leach, M., & Newell, P. (2015). (eds). *The Politics of Green Transformations.* Abingdon: Routledge.

Scoones, I., Stirling, A., Abrol, D. et al. (2020). 'Transformations to sustainability: combining structural, systemic and enabling approaches'. *Current Opinion in Environmental Sustainability*, 42, 65–75.

SEI et al. (2020). *The Production Gap*. UNEP & SEI. https://productiongap.org/wp-content/uploads/2020/12/PGR2020_FullRprt_web.pdf

Semenza, J., Ploubidis, G., & George, L. (2011). 'Climate change and climate variability: personal motivation for adaptation and mitigation'. *Environmental Health*, 10(1): 46–58. https://doi.org/10.1186/1476-069x-10-46

Seyfang, G. (2006). 'Ecological citizenship and sustainable consumption: Examining local organic food networks'. *Journal of Rural Studies*, 22, 383–395.

Shepherd, L., O'Carroll, R. E., & Ferguson, E. (2014). 'An international comparison of deceased and living organ donation/transplant rates in opt-in and opt-out systems: a panel study'. *BMC Medicine*, 12(1), 131.

Shove, E. (2010). 'Beyond the ABC: Climate change policy and theories of social change'. *Environment and Planning A*, 42(6), 1273–1285.

Shove, E. (2003). *Comfort, Cleanliness and Convenience: The Social Organization of Normality*. Oxford: Berg Publishers.

Shove, E., Pantzar, M., & Watson, M. (2012). *The Dynamics of Social Practice: Everyday Life and How it Changes*. London: Sage.

Shove, E. & Walker, G. (2010). 'Governing transitions in the sustainability of everyday life'. *Research Policy*, 39(4), 471–476. https://doi.org/10.1016/j.respol.2010.01.019

Sikor, T. & Newell, P. (2014). 'Globalizing environmental justice?', *Geoforum*, 54, 151–157.

Simms, A. (2010). *21 Hours: Why a Shorter Working Week can help us All to Flourish in the 21st Century*. London: NEF.

Simms, A. (2013). *Cancel the Apocalypse: New Pathways to Prosperity*. London: Little Brown.

Simms, A. (2019). *Climate and Rapid Behaviour Change: What do we know so far?* Rapid Transition Alliance. Available at: https://www.rapidtransition.org/resources/climate-rapid-behaviour-change-what-do-we-know-so-far/

Sitra. (2020). Pathways to 1.5-degree Lifestyles by 2030. Helsinki: Sitra. www.sitra.fi/en/publications/pathways-to-1-5-degree-lifestyles-by-2030/.

Sleeth-Keppler, D., Perkowitz, R., & Speiser, M. (2017). 'It's a matter of trust: American judgments of the credibility of informal communicators on solutions to climate change'. *Environmental Communication*, 11(1), 17–40, http://doi.org/10.1080/17524032.2015.1062790

Smith, S. R., Christie, I., & Willis, R. (2020). 'Social tipping intervention strategies for rapid decarbonization need to consider how change happens'.

Letter in Proceedings of the National Academy of Sciences, 2020, 202002331. https://doi.org/10.1073/pnas.2002331117

Solovjew-Wartiovaara, A. (2021). *Futures Barometer: The Coronavirus has Affected Finns' Prospects for the Future – People's Faith in the Future depends Heavily on their Livelihood.* Sitra: Helsinki. www.sitra.fi/en/news/futures-barometer-the-coronavirus-has-affected-finns-prospects-for-the-future-peoples-faith-in-the-future-depends-heavily-on-their-livelihood/

Soper, K. (2020). *Post-Growth Living: For an Alternative Hedonism.* London: Verso.

Sorrell, S., Dimitropoulos, J., & Sommerville, M. (2009). 'Empirical estimates of the direct rebound effect: A review'. *Energy Policy,* 37(4), 1356–1371.

Sorrell, S., Gatersleben, B., & Druckman, A., (2020). 'The limits of energy sufficiency: A review of the evidence for rebound effects and negative spillovers from behavioural change'. *Energy Research & Social Science,* 64, 101439.

Southerton, D. (2013). 'Habits, routines and temporalities of consumption: From individual behaviours to the reproduction of everyday practices'. *Time & Society,* 22(3), 335–355.

Sovacool, B. K. (2016). 'How long will it take? Conceptualizing the temporal dynamics of energy transitions'. *Energy Research & Social Science,* 13, 202–215.

Sovacool, B. K. (2021) 'Who are the victims of low-carbon transitions? Towards a political ecology of climate change mitigation'. *Energy Research & Social Science,* 73 (2021), 101916.

Sovacool, B. K. & Griffiths, S. (2020). 'The cultural barriers to a low-carbon future: A review of six mobility and energy transitions across 28 countries'. *Renewable and Sustainable Energy Reviews,* 119, 109569.

Sovacool, B. K., Kester, J., Noel, L., & de Rubens, G. Z. (2018). 'The demographics of decarbonizing transport: The influence of gender, education, occupation, age, and household size on electric mobility preferences in the Nordic region'. *Global Environmental Change,* 52, 86–100.

Sovacool, B. K. & Martiskainen, M. (2020). 'Hot transformations: Governing rapid and deep household heating transitions in China, Denmark, Finland and the United Kingdom'. *Energy Policy,* 139, 111330.

Sovacool, B. K, Turnheim, B., Martiskainen, M., Brown, D., & Kivimaa, P. (2020). 'Guides or gatekeepers? Incumbent-oriented transition intermediaries in a low-carbon era'. *Energy Research & Social Science,* 66, 101490.

Spangenberg, J. & Lorek, S. (2019). 'Sufficiency and consumer behaviour: From theory to policy'. *Energy Policy,* 129, 1070–1079. http://doi.org/10.1016/j.enpol.2019.03.013

Spence, A. & Pidgeon, N. (2009). 'Psychology, climate change & sustainable behaviour'. *Environment: Science and Policy for Sustainable Development*, 51(6), 8–18.

Stephenson, J., Barton, B., Carrington, G. et al. (2010). 'Energy cultures: A framework for understanding energy behaviours'. *Energy Policy*, 38(10), 6120–6129.

Stern, P. C., Janda, K. B., Brown, M. A. et al. (2016). 'Opportunities and insights for reducing fossil fuel consumption by households and organizations'. *Nature Energy*, 1(5), 1–6.

Stone, J. (2021). Spain set to pilot four-day week as response to coronavirus pandemic. *The Independent*. Retrieved 29 January 2021, from www.inde pendent.co.uk/news/world/politics/spain-covid-four-dayweek-pilot-b1794322.html.

Stokkard, I. et al. (2021). 'Three decades of climate mitigation: why haven't we bent the global emissions curve?' *Annual Review of Environment and Natural Resources*, 46, 653–689.

Supran, G. & Oreskes, N. (2021). 'Rhetoric and frame analysis of ExxonMobil's climate change communications'. *One Earth*. 4(5), 696–719.

Swyngedouw, E. (2010). 'Apocalypse forever?' *Theory, Culture & Society*, 27 (2–3), 213–232. http://doi.org/10.1177/0263276409358728

Tàbara, J., Lieu, J., Zaman, R., Ismail, C., & Takama, T. (2021). 'On the discovery and enactment of positive socio-ecological tipping points: insights from energy systems interventions in Bangladesh and Indonesia'. *Sustainability Science*. http://doi.org/10.1007/s11625-021-01050-6

Taylor, D. (2021). 'Free parking for free people: German road laws and rights as constraints on local car parking management'. *Transport Policy*, 101, 23–33. http://doi.org/10.1016/j.tranpol.2020.11.013

Thaler, R. H. & Sunstein, C. R. (2009). *Nudge: Improving Decisions about Health, Wealth, and Happiness*. London: Penguin.

Thunberg, G., Neubauer, L., De Wever, A., & Charlier, A. (2020). 'After two years of school strikes, the world is still in a state of climate crisis denial'. *The Guardian*. Retrieved 8 September 2020, from www.theguardian.com/com mentisfree/2020/aug/19/climate-crisis-leaders-greta-thunberg.

Thøgersen, J. (1999). 'Spillover processes in the development of a sustainable consumption pattern'. *Journal of Economic Psychology*, 20, 53–81.

Thøgersen, J. & Alfinito, S. (2020). 'Goal activation for sustainable consumer choices: A comparative study of Denmark and Brazil'. *Journal of Consumer Behaviour*, 2020, 1–14.

Thøgersen, J. & Noblet, C. (2012). 'Does green consumerism increase the acceptance of wind power?' *Energy Policy*, 51, 854–862.

Thøgersen, J. & Schrader, U. (2012). 'From knowledge to action – New paths towards sustainable consumption'. *Journal Of Consumer Policy*, 35(1), 1–5. https://doi.org/10.1007/s10603-012-9188-7

Tollefson, J. (2021). 'COVID curbed carbon emissions in 2020 – but not by much'. *Nature*, 589(7842), 343–343. http://doi.org/10.1038/d41586-021-00090-3

Tosun, J. & Schoenefeld, J. (2016). 'Collective climate action and networked climate governance'. *Wires Climate Change*, 8(1): 1–17. http://doi.org/10.1002/wcc.440

Trades Union Congress [TUC]. (2020). It's shocking that there's now a million people on zero-hours contracts. Tweet retrieved on 11th August, from: https://twitter.com/The_TUC/status/1293104114612699136?ref_src=twsrc%5Egoogle%7Ctwcamp%5Eserp%7Ctwgr%5Etweet

Trainer, T. (1995). *The Conserver Society: Alternatives for Sustainability*. London: Zed Books.

Tukker, A., Cohen, M. J., Hubacek, K., & Mont, O. (2010). 'The impacts of household consumption and options for change'. *Journal of Industrial Ecology*, 14, 13–30.

United Nations Environment Programme [UNEP]. (2005). *Talk the Walk: Advancing Sustainable Lifestyles through Marketing and Communications*. Paris: United Nations Environment Programme.

United Nations Environment Programme [UNEP]. (2020). *Emissions Gap Report 2020*. Nairobi.

United Nations Environment Programme [UNEP]. (2021). *Emissions Gap Report 2021*. Nairobi.

Unruh, G. (2000). 'Understanding carbon lock-in'. *Energy Policy*, 28(12), 817–830. http://doi.org/10.1016/s0301-4215(00)00070-7

Urry, J., (2010). 'Consuming the planet to excess'. *Theory, Culture & Society*, 27(2–3), 191–212.

Van den Berg, N. J., van Soest, H. L., Hof, A. F. et al. (2020). 'Implications of various effort-sharing approaches for national carbon budgets and emission pathways'. *Climatic Change* 162, 1805–1822.

Vandenbergh, M. P. & Sovacool, B. K. (2016). 'Individual behaviour, the social sciences and climate change'. In Faure, M. (ed) *Elgar Encyclopedia of Environmental Law* (pp. 92-102). Edward Elgar.

Van Vuuren, D., Stehfest, E., Gernaat, D. et al. (2018). 'Alternative pathways to the 1.5 °C target reduce the need for negative emission technologies'. *Nature Climate Change*, 8(5), 391-397.

Wallace-Wells, D. (2019). *The Uninhabitable Earth: Life after warming*. London: Tim Duggan Books.

Warde, A. (2014). 'After taste: Culture, consumption and theories of practice'. *Journal of Consumer Culture*, 14, 279–303.

Webb, J., Stone, L., Murphy, L., & Hunter J. (2021). *The Climate Commons: How Communities can Thrive in a Climate Changing World*. Institute for Public Policy Research: UK. www.ippr.org/research/publications/the-climate-commons

Weintrobe, S. (ed.). (2013). *Engaging with Climate Change: Psychoanalytic and Interdisciplinary Perspectives*. Abingdon: Routledge.

Westley, F. & Antadze, N. (2010). 'Making a difference: Strategies for scaling social innovation for greater impact'. *Innovation Journal*, 15(2): 1–19.

Westley, F., Olsson, P., Folke, C. et al. (2011). 'Tipping toward sustainability: emerging pathways of transformation'. *Ambio*, 40(7), 762.

White, K., Habib, R., & Hardisty, D. J. (2019a). 'How to SHIFT consumer behaviors to be more sustainable: A literature review and guiding framework'. *Journal of Marketing*, 83(3), 22-49.

White, K., Hardisty, D. J., & Habib, R. (2019b). 'The elusive green consumer'. *Harvard Business Review*, 11:. 124–133.

Whitmarsh, L. (2009). 'Behavioural responses to climate change: asymmetry of intentions and impacts'. *Journal of Environmental Psychology*, 29, 13–23.

Wiedmann, T., Lenzen, M., Keyßer, L., & Steinberger, J. (2020). 'Scientists' warning on affluence'. *Nature Communications*, 11(1). https://doi.org/10.1038/s41467-020-16941-y

Wilhite, H. (2016). *The Political Economy of Low Carbon Transformation*. Abingdon: Routledge.

Wilkinson, R. & Pickett, L. (2009). *The Spirit Level: Why Equality Is Better for Everyone*. London: Allen Lane.

Willett, W., Rockström, J., Loken, B. et al. (2019). 'Food in the Anthropocene: the EAT–Lancet commission on healthy diets from sustainable food systems'. *Lancet*. 2019; (published online January 16.) http://dx.doi.org/10.1016/S0140-6736(18)31788-4

Williamson, K., Satre-Meloy, A., Velasco, K., & Green, K. (2018). *Climate Change Needs Behavior Change: Making the Case For Behavioral Solutions to Reduce Global Warming*. Arlington, VA: Rare.

Willis, R. (2018). 'Constructing a 'representative claim' for action on climate change: Evidence from interviews with politicians'. *Political Studies*, 66(4), 940–958.

Willis, M. M. & Schor, J. B. (2012). 'Does changing a light bulb lead to changing the world? Political action and the conscious consumer'. *The ANNALS of the American Academy of Political and Social Science*, 644(1), 160–190.

Woiwode, C., Schäpke, N., Bina, O. et al. (2021). 'Inner transformation to sustainability as a deep leverage point: fostering new avenues for change through dialogue and reflection'. *Sustainability Science* (16), 841–858.

World Bank. (2020). Poverty Overview. Retrieved 26 May 2021, from www .worldbank.org/en/topic/poverty/overview

Zhang, R. & Zhang, J. (2021). 'Long-term pathways to deep decarbonization of the transport sector in the post-COVID world'. *Transport Policy*, 110, 28–36. http://doi.org/10.1016/j.tranpol.2021.05.018

Zhong, C. B., Ku, G., Lount, R. B., & Murnighan, J. K. (2010). 'Compensatory ethics'. *Journal of Business Ethics*, 92(3), 323–339.

Acknowledgements

We are immensely grateful to the KR foundation for supporting the research and the work of the *Cambridge Sustainability Commission on Scaling Behaviour Change,* whose work underpins this Element. In particular, we would like to thank Kate Power for her guidance and support for the Commission and encouragement to produce its findings in this series. We would like to thank the 31 members of the *Cambridge Sustainability Commission on Scaling Behaviour Change* for their time, expertise, and insights which fed into this work and to the input of the Boundless Roots community of sustainable living practitioners. We are grateful to Professors Aarti Gupta and Frank Biermann for their encouragement to write this Element. Finally, we would like to thank our partners and families for their forbearance and support in bringing this project to fruition.

About the Authors

Peter Newell is a Professor of International Relations at the University of Sussex and co-founder and research director of the Rapid Transition Alliance. His recent research focuses on the political economy of low-carbon energy transitions, but he has undertaken research, advocacy, and consultancy work on different aspects of climate change for over 25 years. He has worked at the universities of Sussex, Oxford, Warwick, and East Anglia in the United Kingdom where he was Professor of Development Studies, and FLACSO Argentina. He also sits on the board of directors of Greenpeace UK and is a member of the advisory board of the Greenhouse think-tank. He serves on the board of the journals *Global Environmental Politics, Journal of Peasant Studies, European Journal of International Relations and the Earth Systems Governance Journal*. His single and co-authored books include *Climate for Change; The Effectiveness of EU Environmental Policy; Governing Climate Change; Globalization and the Environment: Capitalism, Ecology and Power; Climate Capitalism; Transnational Climate Change Governance; Global Green Politics* and *Power Shift: The Global Political Economy of Energy Transitions*.

Freddie Daley is a Research Associate at the University of Sussex and a Research Co-ordinator for the Fossil Fuel Non-Proliferation Treaty. His research focuses on sustainable behaviour change, supply-side mitigation policy, and energy transitions. He has published in the journal *Global Sustainability*, co-authored the report of the *Cambridge Sustainability Commission on Scaling Behaviour Change* and is author of the *Fossil Fuelled 5* report exploring the role of wealthy nations in expanding fossil fuel production and exports.

Michelle Twena is a Research Associate at the University of Sussex. She has a PhD in EU environmental policymaking from the University of East Anglia, UK, and has published on a range of topics exploring climate and environmental governance and policy, with a particular focus on institutional innovation, experimental learning, and transformation. She has worked at the Center for International Climate Research in Oslo, Norway (CICERO), the Tyndall Centre for Climate Change, University of East Anglia, UK, and CARE International, Dar es Salaam, where she has undertaken research on climate impacts, mitigation and adaptation, international climate negotiations and agreements, climate-poverty reduction strategies, and social exclusion, for the European Commission, Norwegian Research Council, and Norwegian Ministries for the Environment and Foreign Affairs.

Cambridge Elements ☰

Earth System Governance

Frank Biermann

Utrecht University

Frank Biermann is Research Professor of Global Sustainability Governance with the Copernicus Institute of Sustainable Development, Utrecht University, the Netherlands. He is the founding Chair of the Earth System Governance Project, a global transdisciplinary research network launched in 2009; and Editor-in-Chief of the new peer-reviewed journal *Earth System Governance* (ElseviSer). In April 2018, he won a European Research Council Advanced Grant for a research program on the steering effects of the Sustainable Development Goals.

Aarti Gupta

Wageningen University

Aarti Gupta is Professor of Global Environmental Governance at Wageningen University, The Netherlands. She is Lead Faculty and a member of the Scientific Steering Committee of the Earth System Governance (ESG) Project and a Coordinating Lead Author of its 2018 Science and Implementation Plan. She is also principal investigator of the Dutch Research Council-funded TRANSGOV project on the Transformative Potential of Transparency in Climate Governance. She holds a PhD from Yale University in environmental studies.

Michael Mason

London School of Economics and Political Science (LSE)

Michael Mason is Associate Professor in the Department of Geography and Environment at the London School of Economics and Political Science (LSE). At LSE he is also the Director of the Middle East Centre and an Associate of the Grantham Institute on Climate Change and the Environment. Alongside his academic research on environmental politics and governance, he has advised various governments and international organisations on environmental policy issues, including the European Commission, ICRC, NATO, the UK Government (FCDO), and UNDP.

About the Series

Linked with the Earth System Governance Project, this exciting new series will provide concise but authoritative studies of the governance of complex socio-ecological systems, written by world-leading scholars. Highly interdisciplinary in scope, the series will address governance processes and institutions at all levels of decision-making, from local to global, within a planetary perspective that seeks to align current institutions and governance systems with the fundamental 21st Century challenges of global environmental change and earth system transformations.

Elements in this series will present cutting edge scientific research, while also seeking to contribute innovative transformative ideas towards better governance. A key aim of the series is to present policy-relevant research that is of interest to both academics and policy-makers working on earth system governance.

More information about the Earth System Governance project can be found at: www.earthsystemgovernance.org.

Cambridge Elements ≡

Earth System Governance

Elements in the Series

Deliberative Global Governance
John S. Dryzek, Quinlan Bowman, Jonathan Kuyper, Jonathan Pickering,
Jensen Sass and Hayley Stevenson

Environmental Rights in Earth System Governance: Democracy Beyond Democracy
Walter F. Baber and Robert V. Bartlett

The Making of Responsible Innovation
Phil Macnaghten

Environmental Recourse at the Multilateral Development Banks
Susan Park

Remaking Political Institutions: Climate Change and Beyond
James J. Patterson

Forest Governance: Hydra or Chloris?
Bas Arts

Decarbonising Economies
Harriet Bulkeley, Johannes Stripple, Lars J. Nilsson, Bregje van Veelen,
Agni Kalfagianni, Fredric Bauer and Mariësse van Sluisveld

Changing Our Ways: Behaviour Change and the Climate Crisis
Peter Newell, Freddie Daley and Michelle Twena

A full series listing is available at www.cambridge.org/EESG